Bunches and Piles and Heaps...Oh My!

Bunches and Piles and Heaps...Oh My!

AN AUTOBIOGRAPHY OF A CANCER SURVIVOR

• • •

Sharon E. Sirocco

ISBN: 1539145425
ISBN 13: 9781539145424
Library of Congress Control Number: 2016916406
CreateSpace Independent Publishing Platform
North Charleston, South Carolina

Dedication page

• • •

It has always been incredibly difficult for me to ask for and/or receive assistance.

Mainly because I had always been independent and healthy and able to care for my own needs. But time and circumstances have a way of changing things. Today, I am so thankful for the simplest acts of assistance, whether it be holding a door open, carrying a package, helping me up or down stairs, or handing me a needed item from the top shelf of a grocery store. To you who have assisted me in any way, thank you!

To my "prayer warriors" who have and continue to pray for me daily, and to those of you who have showered me with cards of encouragement, thank you!

To the many medical professionals who have cared for me, thank you!

To my sisters, Donna and Julie, and brother-in-law, Darrell: Thank you for being my back-up support team; always ready and willing to lend a hand at night and on weekends when you were home from work. Thank you and I love you!

However, to Mama, Daddy, Jacob, and Justin who have to contend with me 24/7;

I dedicate this book to you! You will never know the love I have for each of you. Although I know my "handicap" has caused your lifestyles to change drastically, you respond with, "What handicap?" You encourage me to be independent, but you also sense my needs and supply them even before I ask. You fill our home with laughter, each in your own "unique" way; sometimes with silly songs, a corny joke or teasing me about my southern drawl. Most importantly, Mama and Daddy, you have made it evident that our household serves the Lord. Thank you!

To my Lord and Savior, Jesus Christ, my life will continue to be dedicated to you forever. Thank you for making this book possible and may it be a testimony to its readers that You alone are *"the way, the truth and the life." John 14:6.*

Contents Page

Foreword

• • •

IN 1985, A JOY CAME into my life and the life of the Lynchburg Rheumatology Clinic (LRC). Sharon Sirocco was hired as our transcriptionist. What a humble beginning for someone who would become our indispensable office manager. Over the next twenty-five years, her continuous desire to gain more knowledge and help us adapt to changes in the business operations of a medical office resulted in Sharon becoming a certified coder, notary public, in-house IT expert, human resource manager, and book keeper. She even completed a course for medical office management. We once counted thirty items she had to oversee on a daily basis.

During this time, she endeared herself to all of us. She was given pet names: Sweet Pea, Little Chicken, Munchkin (my favorite), and The Rock. We joked that the last name referred to her improved bone density or the highest vitamin D level in the office. "The Rock" could have related to her toughest job -- bringing me bad news as rent or overhead went up and Medicare compensation decreased. But, it represents much more.

I remember the night in October 1994 when she called preparing to go to MCV for her kidney and pancreas transplant. She was understand-ably apprehensive, but you could sense her strong faith and courage as she left for Richmond starting this great adventure. After the transplant, she experienced problems with osteoporotic stress fractures. In spite of the pain, her spirit and determination to return to work were remarkable to witness. Sharon has been more like "The Rock" Simon Peter -- a strong faith base on which LRC rested.

She is an essential part of the religion and spirituality health ministry that developed in our office. A sermon I heard several years ago made the point that sometimes the only religion or faith some people experience is what they witness in others. In the book that follows, the reader will witness a remarkable faith tested by recurrent cancer, chemotherapy failures, complicated surgeries, and difficult rehabilitation.

Although LRC closed December 31, 2010, our LRC staff continues as "extended family." Through these years of complicated medical problems, Sharon frequently kept us informed by email. Even when the news was bad, her faith was evidenced by this closing message -- "God is good." Her faith statement is part of the joy she brought to our office and now shares with you, the reader, in her story.

Jeffrey W. Wilson, M.D.

Jeffrey W. Wilson, M.D.

CHAPTER 1

Cabbage Patch Kid

• • •

"There is a time for everything, and a season
for every activity under the heavens"

...ECCLESIASTES 3:1

IT WAS SUNDAY, OCTOBER 9, 1994. Beep, beep, beep...then silence. Beep, beep, beep...then reality set in. It was my pager notifying me that the Medical College of Virginia wanted me to give them a call. Why was I wearing a pager? Why did MCV want me to call? The answer to these questions, and much more, is the reason I am going to try to share my life's story with you.

My life is a testimony to the fact that God still works miracles, heals, and always hears our many prayers. I want to give Him all the praise, honor, and glory for the miracles He has performed in my life. If sharing what God has done for me can give hope and encouragement to even one person; then the many hours that it took me to write this book will be worth it all.

So, let's go back in time and get started. Donald and Margo Sirocco proudly announce the birth of a baby girl, Sharon Elizabeth Sirocco, on May 12, 1964 at 1:14 P.M., weighing 8 lbs. 14 oz. Hey, that's me...a healthy baby girl! Although I was born in Lynchburg, VA, I was lovingly told that I was found in a cabbage patch. Guess that made me a "cabbage patch kid" long before they were ever marketed. Mama said that I was a happy baby and only cried when I was hungry or alone. So, to keep me pacified, Mama would put me in my infant seat and sit it wherever she was working.

As I grew older, you could still find me wherever Mama was. If she was washing dishes, sometimes I would just sit in the floor in front of the refrigerator and watch. I remember a green apron that Mama wore around the house. It had two big pockets at the bottom and I would put my feet in those pockets, wrap my arms around her neck, and off she would go to do her chores with me hanging on. I was happy when I was with my Mama – and some things never change!

When I got a little older, I liked helping my Daddy when he would cut wood. I had a ruler and a yellow marking pen to mark the log in just the right spot so Daddy would know where to cut it. I honestly thought I was helping him. I didn't think he could do it without me!

As the years passed and I thought about my "special job", it dawned on me that Daddy knew exactly what he was doing. He didn't need me to show him where to cut the log, but he made me feel important and gave me a job to do so he could spend time with his little girl even when he was working.

Remember, I told you that my life has been filled with miracles. Just listen to this: I was with my Daddy one day getting ready to do my "job" of marking those logs, but he told me he had to cut a tree down first. He gave me specific instructions telling me exactly where to stand and strict orders not to move until the tree was down. I stood exactly where he told me to, however, the tree did not fall where Daddy had planned, but fell in the opposite direction right where I was standing. Daddy said he just froze as he watched that tree fall, not knowing if I would be seriously injured or possibly dead. When the tree came to rest on the ground, there I was -- still standing exactly where Daddy told me to, with only my head visible among the tree branches, but not one scratch on me. Coincidence? I don't think so! A miracle? I know so! *"For I know the plans I have for you," says the Lord. "They are plans for good and not for disaster, to give you a future and a hope." Jeremiah 29:11*

My neighborhood was full of boys; not a single girl my age for me to play with. Now how do you remedy that situation? You don't...you just make the best of the situation at hand and join in with the boys. I turned into one of the biggest tomboys you have ever seen. At Christmas time, I didn't ask for Barbie dolls or any type of girlie stuff; just give me a new football or basketball, some new jeans and a pair of hiking boots.

I could keep up with any boy in the neighborhood riding bikes, playing basketball and even football. Most of the time, we played flag football, but at times the boys wanted to play tackle. I guess they thought they would leave me out of the game if they played tackle...wrong!!! I will have to say that they didn't tackle me as hard as they did each other. They would sort of pick me up and sit me down gently on the ground.

Like all "boys", I had cap guns and holsters and a space gun to keep the Martians from invading our territory. We would play outside all day, only taking time out for a quick lunch. We took turns going to our different houses to play and our parents had no fear for our safety. At night, we continued to get together to play hide-and-seek or kick the can. What a different life style we had compared to the children of today.

CHAPTER 2

I'm a Little "Pee Pot"

• • •

MY SCHOOL YEARS BEGAN AND I attended a private kindergarten in Madison
Heights, VA because there were no kindergarten classes in the public
schools at that time (1969). My elementary years were spent at Colony
Road School in grades one through three and continued at Phelps Road
Elementary School for grades four through seven. I loved going to school,
at least for the first several years. However, between age seven and eight,
some subtle changes in my life took place and going to school was no longer
the joy it had once been. Why; you might wonder? Let me try to explain.

If you lived in or around Lynchburg, VA, you will certainly remember
Pittman Plaza, Lynchburg's first shopping center. Most Friday nights,
our family would get ready to "go to town", as we called it, and usually our
first stop would be Pittman Plaza, which was only about six miles from our
home. Mama would always make sure that we went to the bathroom before we left home. I would pee before leaving, but by the time we reached
the Plaza, I would have to pee again. Sometimes I would have to go more
than once before we got back home. No one else in the family ever had to
go to the bathroom while we were away. What was wrong with me? As
this same scenario continued time after time, Mama began to ask herself
the same question -- "What IS wrong with her?"

That question needed to be answered, so I was taken to my pediatrician
to see if I might have a bladder or kidney disorder. All tests were negative.
Tests for diabetes were done, negative as well. As my problem continued
to plague me; there were more trips to the doctor, more tests, and more
negative results. The months turned into a year and this urgency to pee

every hour continued with seemingly no solution. The next time you see the TV commercial showing a bladder dragging a woman off to the bathroom everywhere she goes; picture my face on that woman -- that was me for sure.

Finally, my pediatrician decided to admit me to the hospital for more extensive tests; the first being a six-hour glucose tolerance test to check once again for diabetes. I was given glucose intravenously and as the hours ticked away, my blood sugar began to rise. By the end of the test, it had reached almost 600. No mistaking the diagnosis now; I had juvenile diabetes. I continued my stay in the hospital for a few days to learn how to give myself insulin shots and how I could still live a normal life with diabetes. My doctor now understood why my previous blood sugar tests had always been negative. They were always done in the morning when my blood sugar was usually normal. It was late evening when my blood sugar would go up.

After a few days, I got to go home, but my lifestyle would have to change considerably. My daily routine would now consist of insulin shots, monitoring my blood sugar level morning and night, and eating healthy meals, along with snacks in between. No sugar!!! The shots weren't that bad. Even not being able to have sweets didn't bother me that much. What I didn't like about the whole situation was the thought that I was "different". I had never known anyone with diabetes. In fact, I'm not sure if I had ever heard the word, "diabetes". "Mama, I just don't want anyone to know." She agreed that for the time being, I did not have to tell anyone except my teachers. They would need to be aware in the event that my blood sugar dropped too low while I was at school. But, slowly the word trickled out and I felt like the whole world knew my "secret".

The next several years were good ones. Hey, this diabetes stuff was not so bad! I would take my insulin and eat pretty much what I wanted, except for sweets. I took part in school activities, played clarinet in the school band starting in fifth grade, and played Little League ball on the boys' team. In fact, one of my good friends and I were the first two girls ever to play on a boys' team in Madison Heights. Believe it or not, in 1974, our team was American League Champs. Hooray for the girls.

In 7th grade, I had my first insulin reaction. I had gone to spend the night with a friend and we went shopping at the Plaza that night. We both bought a pair of Levi's jeans; boy's Levi's mind you, with a red tag on the back pocket. We had "arrived". We were part of the "in" crowd, or so we thought. We had plans to go to the ball field the next day to check out all of the cute guys. Before going to bed that night, we talked and talked and tried to decide what kind of top would look the coolest with those new jeans. Then, it was lights out and off to sleep to dream of what we had planned. Well, as often is the case, things didn't work out as we had planned.

When I woke up the next morning, I was at home in my own bed with no recollection of anything that had happened. Sometime during the night, my parents had been called to come get me because I was trembling and seemed to be in a semi-conscious state. I had actually just had my first seizure because my blood sugar had dropped too low. A weird experience to say the least. Oh, by the way, we did go to the ball field to check out those cute guys.

Here comes another one! I was in the 7th grade and I was supposed to be taking an English test. When it was time to turn the test in, I walked to the teacher's desk, handed her my paper, and then just stood there. When the teacher looked at my paper, there were no legible words on it, just squiggly lines going across the page. She looked up at me and realized that I was in "another world". Thank God, she knew what to do and sent someone to get me some orange juice. I didn't want to have another experience like that, so it was off to the doctor to find out what had caused my trip into "outer space". Thankfully, there was a simple solution; I just needed to make some adjustments in the amount of insulin to take and make sure that I ate a snack between meals. I could do that! Then, school was out for the summer and I did not have any problems throughout those months, praise God! *Philippians 4:19 "And this same God who takes care of me will supply all your needs from his glorious riches, which have been given to us in Christ Jesus."*

CHAPTER 3
Tween Years

• • •

PHELPS ROAD SCHOOL ONLY WENT through the 7th grade, so in the fall I would be transferring to Monelison Junior High School. It was a brand new school and would house only 8th and 9th graders. Our 7th grade graduating class from Phelps Road would be one of the first groups to christen it.

My years at Monelison were uneventful health wise. I participated in all of the regular school functions, played clarinet in the school band, and went to my first prom. They passed so quickly, much too quickly for me to feel ready to move on to the high school. I had grown so comfortable being with my friends in middle school, but now I would become the "new kid on the block". Mama reminded me that all of my friends were in the same boat, and we just needed to stick together and everything would be all right.

My first few days at the high school were much better than I had anticipated. I had classes with a lot of friends from Monelison and was already making new friends as well. Don't you just hate it when Mama's are always right? I wanted to continue playing the clarinet, so I joined the high school concert band. It was in band class that I met my first "love". We were inseparable throughout my entire junior year. However, as with most first loves, they inevitably come to an end. OK girl, put a little Super Glue on your heart and get on with your life.

Note: This seems to be an appropriate place to interject a biblical phrase that would become my words of consolation for this and so many more future events: *"And it came to pass..."*

It was the beginning of my senior year and school had only been in session for a few weeks. I did not realize that I had a secret admirer waiting in the wings after my breakup with my former boyfriend, until one day I received a dozen red roses with a note asking me for a date. I wasn't sure that I wanted to be involved in another relationship at that point in time, but after receiving roses several more times, I figured that I better go out with the boy before he went broke. So, we dated for over a year and went to the senior prom together.

My high school days came to a close. I graduated with an advanced diploma and received the Ben and Bertha Wailes scholarship for students going into the medical field because my plans were to go to CVCC for an associate's degree in Medical Records.

Outside of high school, I was active in numerous church activities, I worked as a lifeguard at our local pool for several summers, and also worked as one of Santa's elves at the mall. As you may have noticed, I haven't mentioned any problems with my diabetes during high school. That's not to say that I didn't have any, but for the most part, IF I did what I was supposed to, all went well. "If" -- such a small word with such a giant meaning.

So, so, many stories I could write about during this time frame, but in an effort to keep this book from being too long, I'll refrain from most of them. Just have to tell you this one; it's unique and so funny. Remember, I told you that I was a big tomboy. I guess I must have been fourteen or fifteen when I asked Daddy if he would buy me a motorcycle. The answer was not favorable at that time.

However, as luck would have it, in a matter of weeks, one of my neighbors wanted to know if we knew of anyone that would be interested in a blue Honda 90. Did we ever! It was just my size. Now all I needed to do was convince Daddy to buy it. He agreed much too readily. Could it be that he really wanted that bike as much as I did? Whatever the reason, he bought it...oh, what a happy day! I rode that thing all over our property. Up and down hillsides, in and out of wooded areas, and up and down the driveway. I had a ball riding that bike. I agree that I may have gone a little too fast and I guess I should have kept both wheels on the ground at all times, but...

Daddy enjoyed riding it, too, while Mama just watched from the sidelines, probably sending up prayers for our safety. But one day, Mama asked if she could ride. Why not? I showed her what she was supposed to do and she started off pretty good, but all of a sudden...Mama, watch out for that.... tree! She meant to grab the hand brake, but grabbed the gas lever instead, sending her and the bike to the ground. I didn't know how badly she might be hurt, so I ran in the house to get Daddy. He had just finished taking a shower and was not completely dressed, but he didn't think about that. He was so concerned about Mama that he came running down the steps and out of the front door in just his underwear. He tried jumping over the brick retaining wall beside the front porch, but in his haste, one foot did not clear the wall completely.

So, to make a long story short, we ended up taking both Mama and Daddy to the Emergency Room. Daddy had two broken toes and Mama had to wear a sling for several weeks due to a bruised shoulder. Now just listen to this...they sold my motorcycle!!! What a bummer -- it wasn't me that had the wreck. I suppose they were looking out for my own good before I had a chance to be next. Could that have possibly been a "God incident"? *Lamentations 3:25 The LORD is good to those whose hope is in him, to the one who seeks him.*

CHAPTER 4

College, Here I Come

• • •

AFTER GRADUATION, I DID NOT want to go to college. Twelve years of school was enough for me...I thought. After talking it over with my parents, we all agreed that I could look for a job, work for a year or so, and consider college at a later time.

My first job application went to Hardee's in Madison Heights and I was hired immediately. I caught on pretty quickly to operating the cash register and taking orders. I thought I had a pretty neat job and I was just finishing up my first week, when one of my co-workers told me to come with her and she would show me where the cleaning supplies were for the bathrooms. Would you run that by me one more time? Do you mean I've got to clean bathrooms if I continue to work here? Cleaning bathrooms at home was a chore that I always tried to get out of and I certainly didn't want to clean public bathrooms. It didn't take me long to realize that maybe I had made a mistake about college. So, it was goodbye Hardee's and off to Central Virginia Community College -- Harvard on the Hill.

Medical terminology, English courses and transcription were some of my favorite classes, while anatomy/physiology was definitely at the bottom of my list; even more so after the day my professor announced that our next project was going to be dissecting a cat. I had had a cat for most all of my life. I just didn't think I could handle that assignment, so my lab partner agreed to do the actual dissecting while I watched.

I studied hard and received my AAS Degree in Medical Records in June of 1984. Now it was time to join the "real world" and find a job where cleaning bathrooms was not part of my job description. In only one week,

I was asked to fill in at Monelison Family Physicians for six months while two employees were out on maternity leave. That temporary job ended in mid-December.

Then I was offered a position at Lynchburg General Hospital in the Radiology Department as a transcriptionist. I really liked working there, but unfortunately I had to work second shift from 3:30 - midnight. I did not like that! I worked and slept, and worked and slept, and missed being with my family big time. *"I know the plans I have for you"*, says the Lord. And I am so thankful that God was ready to open another door for me.

I failed to mention this point previously: After graduating from CVCC, I had dropped off my resume at various medical offices in the Lynchburg area. Get ready for an upcoming "God incident".

One sunny day in June of 1985, Mama was sitting in the rocking chair on the porch and I was lying in the sun. (That's a big no-no these days!) The phone rang and the office manager for Lynchburg Endocrinology and Rheumatology Clinic asked if I could come in for a job interview. Just listen to this: She told me their office was looking for a transcriptionist and as she was looking through some papers in her desk, she "just so happened" to find my resume. Now I had dropped that resume off an entire year ago. Didn't I tell you a "God incident" was coming? It was no coincidence that she had held on to that resume that long – it was God's perfect timing. She asked if I could come to the office within the next hour for an interview. Sure, why not? So I jumped up, washed the suntan lotion off, put on something that looked halfway decent, and headed for my interview.

I met with the Endocrinologist first and I thought all went well. Then I met with Dr. Jeffrey Wilson, the Rheumatologist. I don't remember much about the interview, but Dr. Wilson made a statement that I will always remember. He told me that his employees were his "extended family" and he was not just looking for a new employee, but a new family member. I must have made a good impression because I was hired, or rather "adopted", into this new family and began my journey with these new "brothers and sisters" on July 1, 1985. *2 Timothy 1:7 "For the spirit God gave us does not make us timid, but gives us power, love and self-discipline."*

CHAPTER 5

Transplanted in More Ways Than One

. . .

IT WAS DURING MY YEARS of employment at Lynchburg Rheumatology Clinic that my health started to deteriorate. At age 29, my blood sugars became uncontrollable. They would rise to as high as 300 and then within thirty minutes, someone would be shoving something sweet down my throat because my sugar had dropped to 50, sending me into "that other world". This continued for months, both at home and at work, until Dr. Wilson suggested that I make an appointment with his friend, Bobby Lockridge, a nephrologist (kidney doctor).

So I took his advice and had my first appointment with Dr. Robert Lockridge in January of 1994. After reviewing my medical history and lab results, his diagnosis was not what I was expecting to hear…end stage renal disease. The next bit of news was even more mind-blowing as well. He thought I would be a good candidate for a kidney/pancreas transplant. It was either that or live on dialysis for the rest of my life. WOW! What a choice. My mind was having a hard time trying to take all of this in…end stage renal disease, dialysis, kidney/pancreas transplant. I left his office, got into my car, and I just lost it and there was no way that I could hold back the tears.

After a few minutes, I got myself back together and headed to my office to pick up some of my things before going home. I can't begin to tell you how surprised I was to see Dr. Wilson's car still there. He normally didn't stay that late. I wondered why he was still there. Was something wrong? Nothing was wrong...he was waiting for me. Again, I couldn't hold back the tears as I tried to tell him what Dr. Lockridge had just explained to me. He just put his arms around me and comforted me as I blubbered. I do believe I remember seeing a few tears roll down Dr. Wilson's face as well. Just another "God incident" as His plan for the next phase of my life was beginning to unfold.

I finally made it home and Mama and Daddy were waiting to hear about my appointment with Dr. Lockridge. The only words I could get out before I started bawling again were: "I need to have a kidney/pancreas transplant." Like me, they were not expecting that kind of news. Dr. Lockridge had not given me any details about the surgery because he wanted my parents to hear the explanation as well. It was the very next day that Mama, Daddy and I met with him after his office hours to learn more about this kidney/pancreas thing in more detail. When he started his presentation, at first he seemed like a drill sergeant as he spurted out fact after fact after fact. But when his presentation was over, his kind and compassionate nature was evident. Then he asked us if we had any concerns and allowed us to drill him with question after question. After much conversation, we were all in agreement that we should proceed to get my name on a transplant waiting list.

I'm not sure how long our consultation lasted, but Dr. Lockridge made no effort to remind us that his office hours were over long ago and it was way past time for him to go home. On our way home, Mama and Daddy both commented on his remarkable knowledge and the fact that not many doctors would have scheduled an after-hours consultation. They were very impressed with him. I had indeed been referred to a very special doctor that I would soon affectionately call "Doc Lok" and who would ultimately become my friend for life. *Deuteronomy 31:8 "It is the LORD who goes before you. He will be with you; he will not leave you or forsake you. Do not fear or be dismayed."*

"Doc Lok"

Now getting your name on a transplant waiting list was no "piece of cake". First, there was a physical examination to determine if you were healthy enough for the transplant. Next would come lots of lab work to gather specific criteria such as blood type, tissue type, etc. Finally, you would wait for an organ donor that matched your specific profile. Yes, that meant that someone had to die in order to give me a chance to have a better life. What a parallel to what Jesus did for all mankind. He suffered and died on a cross to give eternal life to all who will come to Him in repentance and accept Him as Savior and Lord.

Dr. Lockridge suggested that Johns-Hopkins in Baltimore, Maryland would be a good place for us to start. So, Mama, Daddy and I took his advice and headed for Baltimore for a consultation with a transplant team. Lab work was the first order of business. I think the lab techs must have been related to Dracula because they took tube after tube, after tube of my blood, until I began to wonder if I was going to have enough left to get up out of the chair. Next we went to listen to a brief explanation about the actual transplant procedure.

Mama and Daddy were listening carefully and everyone thought I was too, until the nurse asked me a direct question and I didn't respond. That's all it took for her to know that I had slipped into my "other world" because my sugar had dropped, so she quickly got peanut butter, cookies, and Sprite to bring me back to earth. I missed most of what was said during the appointment due to that little incident. However, I was considered as a good candidate for transplantation and was added to their waiting list.

Dr. Lockridge was not satisfied to have my name on just one transplant waiting list; he also wanted my name on the waiting list at the Medical College of Virginia in Richmond. So we were on the move again, this time to MCV. More blood work, more tests, and another consultation with a transplant team. This time I heard what was said. MCV also thought I would be a good transplant candidate and I was placed on their waiting list.

I was given a pager with a designated number to call whenever it started to beep. Now you need to remember that this was 1994, long before the cell phone craze, so when they gave me that pager, I was thrilled and I thought I was cool. The first time it beeped, I thought my heart was going to jump out of my chest. When I called the office, it turned out to be a wrong number. What a letdown! *Psalm 9:9 "The LORD is a stronghold for the oppressed, a stronghold in times of trouble. And those who know your name put their trust in you, for you, O LORD, have not forsaken those who seek you."*

It was Sunday, October 9, 1994 and normally all of us would have been in church. We had been raised to be in church every Sunday, but on this particular day, I just didn't feel like going. My blood sugar was low again and I was having trouble getting it to a normal level and keeping it there. Around 12:30 P.M., as we were fixing lunch, my beeper went off, so I called MCV and this time it was not a wrong number; it was "the call" I had been waiting for. One of the MCV transplant nurses told me that they had a possible donor match and for me to have my bags packed and to be on standby.

When I told Mama and Daddy the news, we all danced around in the kitchen and hugged each other, but suddenly Mama stopped us because the realization had just hit home that while we were celebrating, some family was grieving the loss of a family member. We stopped our celebration and bowed our heads and prayed for that family.

Before doing anything else, I called my Granny and PaPa, Dr. Lockridge, and Dr. Wilson to tell them that a donor may have been found for me. What an emotional day. My anxiety level was through the roof.

Note: Before I go on, I just want to say that my Granny had told me several days earlier that she had dreamed that I was going to get my transplant and everything was going to be all right. My PaPa even went out and bought me an emerald and diamond ring to wear to the hospital, but I didn't get to wear it because it was too large and had to be resized. You can bet it was waiting for me when I got home.

I received several more calls throughout the day from MCV just keeping me updated on all of the tests that were being done to see if the donor organs matched my profile. It was around 10:00 P.M. when I got the final call to let me know the organs were a positive match. The nurse told me to be careful, but to get there as soon as possible. It was so hard saying goodbye to the rest of my family, especially my nephew, Jacob, who was only two at the time. The tears were flowing as we left home -- tears of sadness that I had to leave my family and probably tears of the "unknown" that was still to come.

We were approaching downtown Richmond, headed for MCV, when we had to take a detour due to some road construction. It didn't take long for Daddy to realize that he had somehow missed our exit and he had no idea which way to go. It "just so happened" that there was a police officer parked on the street and Daddy went over and told him of our dilemma. The officer told us to follow him and we got a police escort right to the hospital door. Did you notice I said, "It just so happened?" It didn't "just so happen" -- it was truly another "God incident".

As I entered the hospital doors, I was quickly taken to the transplant unit on the ninth floor for my surgical pre-op. First, I had to take a shower with some special antibacterial stuff. Do you know how long it takes for hot water to make its way to the ninth floor? I don't either, because it never made its way up during my shower. But you have to do what you have to do. What a cold shower that was. Next, came the Go-Lytely, a liquid, fast acting, laxative to clean you out so you wouldn't poop while on the operating table. Man, that stuff was nasty and it took everything I had to keep it down because if I threw it up, I would have to drink some more.

The orderly arrived and told Mama and Daddy that he was going to borrow me for a little while. They promised me that they would not leave the hospital until they saw me again after surgery. I was rolled down the hall and into some little cubby hole and was left there. My guess was that it was some type of holding area before going into the operating room. Oh my! I was beyond scared! But, we had prayed and prayed and now it was time to put everything in God's hands. Finally, I went to sleep.

As Mama and Daddy began their long wait, they watched all of the fast paced activity in the hallway. Soon they saw a man coming down the hallway with a little Coleman cooler on a rolling cart. They thought that he was bringing in my new organs. Wrong! It was a liver -- I got bumped by a liver because there was a shorter time frame in which to transplant that organ or they would lose it. My kidney and pancreas were somewhere in a Coleman cooler on ice and I was still waiting in my cubby hole. Mama and Daddy were notified that my surgery had been put on hold. *Psalm 119:50 My comfort in my suffering is this: Your promise preserves my life.*"

CHAPTER 6

To Surgery and Beyond

• • •

MID-MORNING ON OCTOBER 10, 1994, my parents were finally notified that my surgery had begun. Mama later relayed this story to me: It was cloudy and rainy that day and when she received word that I was in surgery, she stood at the window, watched the rain pour down for a few moments, and then she began to pray – for me, the doctors, nurses, and everyone that would assist during my surgery. As she was praying, the sun, or was it the "Son", came from behind the clouds and shone brightly, but only for a matter of minutes, as if this was God's way of reassuring her that all would go well.

Even more uncanny, when Mama relayed her story to my Granny, she had the very same story to tell. It had also been rainy and cloudy at home. Granny was on her knees praying and the sun, or the "Son", shone brightly and then disappeared almost as quickly as it had appeared. She knew that this was God's reassurance to her that I was going to be all right. What an awesome God we serve!

It was a long, long, surgery. The hospital staff was so kind and comforting to Mama and Daddy as they waited in anticipation of news concerning my surgery. Someone kept them informed frequently about each procedure that was taking place. It was late at night when one of the doctors came out to talk to them with the reassurance that all went well and I was doing fine. Mama and Daddy had been up for about thirty-six hours now, but a promise is a promise and they had promised me that they wouldn't leave until they saw me after surgery. However, when they told the doctor about their promise, he nipped that plan in the bud…no visitors tonight. They were advised that the best thing they could do was to get some rest. They agreed, but bright and early the next morning, they were in my room with me, even though I wasn't fully aware. I didn't learn until much later that they didn't keep their promise, but under the circumstances, it was understandable and I forgave them.

Here's another little tidbit that I didn't learn until much later. Let's rewind to my pre-op time. Do you remember the Go-Lytely laxative that I had to drink? Instead of Go-Lytely, someone must have given me "Go-Later" because it was much later, in fact mid-way through my surgery, that it finally worked and I pooped all over the operating table. Stop laughing -- I couldn't help it; I was asleep. I pity the poor souls who had to clean up that mess as I lay sprawled out on the operating table with my belly cut wide open. Talk about embarrassing! Sure am glad I didn't learn about it until after the fact. Now that embarrassing fact has got to be worth every penny that you paid for this book!!

It took a day or two for me to feel completely awake and as I looked around the room, it seemed that there were a million tubes going in and out of my body. I was hooked up to so many pumps that were constantly beeping and I wondered how in the world anybody could keep up with what each one was for. *What have they done to me? Isaiah 41:10 "So do not fear, for I am with you; do not be dismayed, for I am your God. I will strengthen you and help you; I will uphold you with my righteous right hand."*

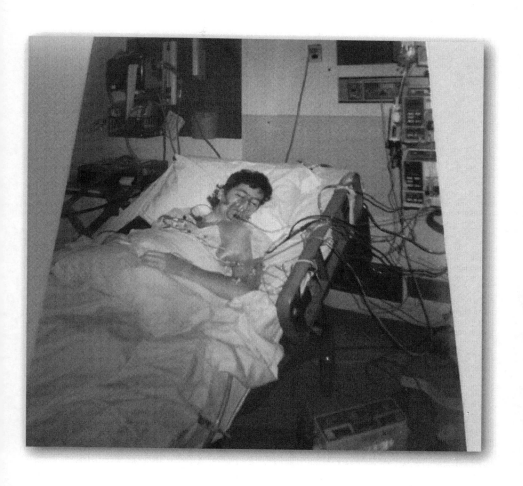

It had been over 48 hours since I had eaten anything and I was hungry. I asked my nurse if I could have something to eat. She brought in my first meal – ice chips!! Maybe it wasn't the hamburger and fries I would have ordered, but they sure did feel good going down. Soon I graduated from ice chips to some real food. One of my nurses brought me a piece of pie and I told her I couldn't eat sweets. Wrong – due to my transplant, those days were history and now I could eat whatever I wanted. I knew that was part of the purpose of the transplant, but I didn't know it would take effect immediately. So, I ate that piece of pie, but I was still somewhat of a "Doubting Thomas", and I asked my nurse if she would please check my blood sugar. Unbelievable, it was normal! Now, that's what I call a miracle! Praise God from whom all blessings flow.

The days had turned into weeks and I was still at MCV. There was little that I could do except watch TV and walk up and down the hallways pushing my IV poles along with me. I had met several other transplant patients while I had been there and sometimes we walked and talked together.

One day as I was taking a stroll, I noticed my preacher, David Vaughan, and his wife, Alberta, coming down the hall toward me. I was so excited to see somebody from "home", but they walked right past me without even speaking. They continued on down the hall and turned into my room, so I knew they had come to see me, but I didn't understand why they didn't speak to me? Now this is too funny...they thought that I was the cleaning lady pushing a cart full of cleaning supplies. Sure enough, I was pushing a bunch of "supplies" down the hall, but they were my IV poles which did hide my face from view quite a bit. We had a good laugh and a nice visit.

David and Alberta Vaughan and the "Cleaning Lady"

Dr. Lockridge, now Doc Lok to me, also came to MCV to visit me and another one of his transplant patients. What a surprise and what a wonderful feeling it gave me to have my doctor drive two and a half hours on his day off just to check on little ol' me. But that was just his nature -- so caring and compassionate and always going "above and beyond the call of duty" for his patients.

CHAPTER 7

Words of Thanksgiving

• • •

FINALLY, THE DAY OF ALL days arrived; the day I was told that I could go home. HOME SWEET HOME...there's no place like home! It didn't take long for me to be all packed and ready to go. *"However"*...sometimes I don't like that word...as the nurse was checking my vital signs before discharging me, she found that I had a slight fever and they would not let me out of those doors. What a letdown! It's for your own good they told me. A fever can sometimes mean that your body is trying to reject the transplanted organs. I know, I know, but I just wanted to go home.

Mama and Daddy continued to stay with me. They had set up a temporary residence at the Shoney's Inn and the manager even gave them special rates due to the circumstances of their month long visit.

A week or so had passed, no fever, no rejection, so soon I would be homeward bound! I was excited, but the day was also bittersweet because I had to say goodbye to so many people that had become my friends: the doctors that made up my transplant team, the nurses, and even the cleaning staff. Thanks for everything!!! Dr. Anne King, Medical Director of the Transplant Unit, would now be my primary care physician and I would have to go back to MCV to see her for my follow up visits.

I have a little problem with car sickness and oh, how I...won't say hated, but extremely disliked that drive to MCV and all of the traffic in the downtown Richmond area. Although I had to travel back and forth to see Dr. King for almost a year, a "God incident" was about to take place. Dr. King and Doc Lok had gone to medical school together and they were good friends. She knew how much I "extremely disliked" traveling back and forth to MCV, so she made arrangements for Doc Lok to do all of my follow up care in Lynchburg. No more traveling back and forth to MCV. What a blessing! Even though I haven't seen Dr. King for a number of years, we remain in touch with each other through e-mail to this day.

Just a few words of thanksgiving before leaving this section of my story: It is October 2016; twenty-two years since my transplant took place. That in itself is unbelievable, but with God, all things are possible.

I want to express my sincere appreciation to my donor family who made my transplant possible. It's only by the grace of God and their decision to give the gift of life, not only to me, but to several other recipients, that I am able to share my thoughts with you in this book. Nothing is a coincidence to me. Everything is part of God's plan and a miracle in my eyes! So again, to my donor family, I am forever grateful to you.

"Without the organ donor, there is no story, no hope, no transplant. But, when there is an organ donor, life springs from death, sorrow turns to hope, and a terrible loss becomes a gift." -- UNOS To my donor family: Thank you for the "gift", the hope, the transplant, and the story! *Ephesians 5:20 "Sing and make music from your heart to the Lord, always giving thanks to God the Father for everything, in the name of our Lord Jesus Christ."*

Home at last! What a wonderful feeling it was to be in my own surroundings with all of my family. It would take me days to catch up on what had been happening while I was away and for me to tell my family about my experiences at MCV. I was feeling great and wanted to go back to work, but the doctors said, just "hold your horses", not just yet. Dr. Wilson was so kind to me. He told me to take as long as I needed and assured me that my job would be waiting for me when I was able to return.

I quickly learned that having a transplant was more than just walking into a hospital, having surgery, and then going about your business. My lifestyle and daily routine changed drastically. I had a truck load of pills to take daily and I needed to have blood work done three times a week for several weeks, then two times, then finally once a week. Doc Lok wanted to keep a good check on my kidney function, etc.

It was during one of my routine blood tests that he saw a slight abnormality and told me to pack my bags for MCV to have a kidney biopsy. I packed my bags as I was told and we headed back to MCV...again. The actual biopsy part wasn't too bad; rather, it was what came after the biopsy. I had to stay flat on my back for four hours with a sand bag over the incision to prevent bleeding. In most cases, four hours is not a very long period of time, but those four hours seemed like an eternity to me.

The results of the biopsy showed some mild rejection to the transplanted organs, meaning I would have to stay in the hospital for treatment, but only for about a week this time. My treatment seemed to be successful and the week passed quickly enough and I was home again and Thanksgiving Day was just around the corner. I had so, so, so much to be thankful for: A new kidney and pancreas that were functioning perfectly, no need for dialysis, normal blood sugar levels, and no longer any need to take insulin shots. I'm one blessed girl! *Psalm 107:15 "Let them give thanks to the Lord for his unfailing love and his wonderful deeds for mankind."*

"Joy to the world, the Lord is come..." time to celebrate the birth of our Lord and Savior, Jesus Christ. There would be lots of family gatherings and special events at church to attend. What a wonderful time of the year! Then, in just days, thousands of people would be gathering in Times Square to watch the giant ball fall, ushering in the New Year 1995. A New Year -- those were exciting words to me; words of hope. I was thrilled to be working full time, going to church, singing in the choir, and doing regular daily activities. Happy New Year to ME!

CHAPTER 8

Dem Dry Bones

• • •

FIVE MONTHS PASSED IN WHAT seemed like the blink of an eye. It was May of 1995, and Mama, Daddy, Jacob and I were off to Myrtle Beach. This had been our family's vacation spot for many years, but it was Jacob's first trip to the beach and it was so much fun just watching him. Maybe I was watching him a little too much instead of watching where I was going, because somewhere along the way, I happened to miss a small step, which made me step down a little harder than usual, causing my right knee to wrench slightly. There was a little pain, but nothing bad enough to keep me from enjoying the rest of our time at the beach. Once we were back at home, I decided to get that knee checked because it was swelling and still painful. You guessed it…I had a broken bone in my knee and would have to be on crutches and non-weight bearing for six weeks.

Boy, did I dread having to tell Dr. Wilson that I would not be able to work for the next six weeks. When I told him of my dilemma, his reply was that I was not going to get out of work that easily and he would be expecting to see me, crutches and all, at the office the next day. My job allowed me to sit at my desk for the most part, but whenever I started to get up, someone would inevitably tell me to sit down and offer to get me whatever I needed. That was just the nature of my extended family -- always looking out for me. After six weeks, I was back on both feet once more. Praise the Lord!

Here's a little history lesson for you at no extra charge: Uncle Billy's Day started in 1949 as a one-day event to commemorate the founding of the Trade Lot where local residents brought their vegetables and live-stock to sell. Uncle Billy Lane, member of the Lane family, founders of the town of Altavista, VA, was steadfast in bringing his goods in a wagon to sell at the Trade Lot and it was named after him for his dedication. Mr. Lane also served as master auctioneer and provided entertainment. The Trade Lot continues to operate the first Saturday of each month as a giant flea market.

Now that you know all about Uncle Billy's Day, that's where we were headed on the first Saturday in June to enjoy all of the activities. We had a good day sampling the food and searching through all the "junque" trying to find that special "treasure". When we got home, Mama noticed that my right foot was a little swollen and also red. There was no pain, so we decided just to keep an eye on it for a couple of days. When it didn't seem to be getting any better, Mama dragged me off to the doctor again.

I was scheduled to see a new doctor that I had never met before. After a brief examination, he said due to the fact that I was able to walk and not having any pain, he thought my problem was "possibly" cellulitis -- note that word "possibly". I was given antibiotics, but after a week or more, my foot actually looked a little worse. A return visit was made to this same "doc" for further evaluation, however the evaluation turned out to be a referral to the Orthopedic Center.

Once at the Ortho Center, x-rays were done and I was anxiously waiting for my usual orthopedic doctor to come in and give me the results. Instead, into my room walked this tall, handsome man who introduced himself as Dr. Eschenroeder and informed me that he would be filling in for my regular doctor who was on vacation. Fine by me. He explained that the top of my foot was crushed and there were several additional broken bones around the ankle. I didn't understand how that could be possible; it didn't hurt and I could still walk. Dr. Eschenroeder explained that due to diabetes, I had developed a condition called Charcot Joint, a syndrome that causes loss of sensation as well as fractures and dislocations of bones and joints with minimal or no known trauma. More surgery, but with a prognosis that was not so favorable – some of the bones may have to be fused, which would cause my ankle to be stiff, but there was no choice in the matter. I would be at the mercy of this surgeon that I had just met for whatever had to be done. God will take care of me...

My surgery had not even been scheduled and already the wheels in my head were turning as to when I might be able to go back to work. Hmmm! My thought was if I had previously been able to work while I was on crutches, I didn't see any reason why I couldn't do it again and go back to work immediately following surgery. But Dr. Wilson's thoughts turned out to be quite different from mine. He felt it would be easier on me to work from home. He was the boss and you don't argue with the boss.

The only drawback of this plan was it would involve Mama or Daddy. One or the other would have to go to the office and pick up dictation tapes for me to transcribe at home and then return the finished work the next day. I didn't like taking their time to travel back and forth for me, but they didn't seem to mind. Working from home really was a blessing. "Dad Wilson" to the rescue once again. Another one of many examples exemplifying Dr. Wilson's love for his "office kids". *John 16:33 "I have said these things to you, that in me you may have peace. In the world you will have tribulation. But take heart; I have overcome the world."*

Many weeks had passed and I was excited that the time had rolled around to have x-rays to check on the healing progression of my foot. Praise God, it was completely healed and I even had some range of motion in my ankle. I was ecstatic about that part, but...my foot looked like something that Dr. Frankenstein might have attached to his "monster". It was so misshapen and a knot protruded from around my ankle that seemed to be the size of a tennis ball. I knew in my heart that everything possible had been done to save my foot, but I wasn't expecting this outcome. Was it going to improve? Well, no. I would have to learn to live with it. Then I thought to myself...self, what in the world are you thinking? "Learn to live with it" ...you should be thankful that you still have that foot no matter what it looks like. I really was thankful, but I guess a little vanity was surfacing.

You see, shoes were always a weakness of mine. I probably had sixty plus pairs that matched each of my outfits and I would never be able to wear them again. Instead, I would need to wear an ugly built-up Frankenstein shoe. Well, I guess since I had a Frankenstein ankle, a Frankenstein shoe shouldn't have been a surprise. Now, wasn't I going to look fashionable!!! Mama tried to convince me that there was no need to keep all of those shoes anymore and she suggested that I just give them away. It took me a while to agree to that, but I knew she was right and we packed them up and away they went.

Enough about shoes, let's get back to some positive facts: Dr. Eschenroeder told me that I could put the crutches away and actually put weight on my foot and...I could go back to work at the office. Let me run that by you one more time -- the doctor said that I could go back to my office. So, I took those words literally and headed for my office which was right next door to the Orthopedic Center. All of my co-workers came and greeted me and then came Dr. Wilson with this cheery greeting -- "break a leg". Now, I had always strived to be a good employee and do as I was told, so I broke a leg -- literally. As I started toward my desk, I heard a pop and my left leg felt unstable, so I just turned around and headed back across the parking lot to the Orthopedic Center and right back into the exam room that I had left just fifteen minutes earlier.

Talk about unbelievable, all I did was walk a short distance. Was this going to be an ongoing pattern every time I tried to walk? By now you know the routine as well as I do: X-rays, etc. At least this time, I was able to have a walking cast, but still had to use the crutches for assistance.

An appointment was made for more x-rays in a couple of weeks, just to make sure the bone was healing properly. Sad to say, it was not and to put it bluntly, I was told the bone would probably never heal on its own. The only solution to keep me from having additional breaks was to insert a metal rod inside of my tibia for support. Ouch! I could just picture my doctor cutting my leg open, sawing my bone apart, and then taking a ten-pound hammer and pounding a metal rod into my bone. Believe it or not, that came close to actually what happened. I remember the anesthesiologist putting me to sleep, but I also remember waking up before the surgery was over. Let me tell you...I felt that metal rod being pounded into my tibia and I was quick to let it be known that I was awake. I heard someone say, "Hang on a little longer; we are almost finished."

What in the world was going on with these bones of mine? I couldn't even walk across the floor without a fracture. One theory was the high doses of Prednisone that I had been taking since my transplant was the culprit. I wasn't all that concerned about the cause, but rather a solution. My greatest fear was there would be no solution.

However, it wasn't too long before I got a call from Doc Lok to tell me that he wanted me to try a bone strengthening drug called Aredia. It would be given intravenously once a month and it would take several months to find out if the treatments were actually working. *Mark 10:27...*" *all things are possible with God.*"

CHAPTER 9

Hip, Hip, Hip, but no Hooray

• • •

I WAS BACK AT WORK once again. I loved my job and I loved being with my extended family. After several months, I thought I had it made. However, on this one particular day, I was not feeling my best, but I managed to make it until closing time. There had been a nagging pain in my left hip all day, so I told my co-workers that I thought I had pulled a muscle and I was going next door to the Ortho Center to see if they could work me in and check it out. My friend, Scarlet, would not let me go alone so we both headed across the parking lot.

As we neared the front door of the building, I collapsed. Scarlet had been walking beside me and as I was going down, she reached out and grabbed me, which helped to break my fall, then ran inside to get help. So there I was, sprawled out on the hot pavement in the parking lot when a gentleman that was leaving the building came over and held an umbrella over me -- thank you, sir.

Note: I had not asked Scarlet to go with me to the Ortho Center, nor had she asked if I wanted her to go. When I left work, she just walked out with me. I wouldn't like to think of what could have happened if she had not been along. Was all of this just a coincidence? No way, but a "God incident" for sure!

Now, I am not a "wimp", and I can stand a lot of pain, but this was the worst pain I had ever had in my entire life. Every time I had to be moved, I wanted to scream out loud and people just kept on moving me from place to place -- from outside to inside, to the x-ray room, to an exam room, into an ambulance, from the ambulance into the hospital, and finally into a bed in my hospital room. The pain was so intense that tears kept streaming down my face. The nurses were finally able to get me propped up in a semi-sitting position that eased the pain somewhat and that's how I stayed the rest of the night. Surgery was scheduled for the next day to put me back together with nuts, bolts, pins, and screws; I couldn't wait. It was successful and soon I was back home recuperating.

The time had come for me to drop in at the office, throw my hat in the door, and wait to see if it would be thrown back at me. As usual, I was welcomed back with lots of hugs. Any other office in town would have fired me by now. I had been back at work for about a month with no incidents, but that same hip sure was hurting for no apparent reason...no falls, no bumps, no "nothing". With my past history, I knew that I needed to have it checked, so here we go again.

I'm not going to go through the whole routine again because I'm sure you know it by now. Let me just give you a brief synopsis of my diagnosis: The screws that were used to hold my hip together were too long and had worked their way through my hip and were rubbing against another bone.

Well, how did they plan to remedy that? No problem – they would just go back in and remove the long screws and put in some shorter ones. No problem for them maybe, but it was my leg that was going to be cut into again.

Supposedly, all would be well after this surgery. Wrong!!! It didn't take long for the pain to return in the same area. Why? This time the screws were too short and were not holding the bones together securely. (It's all right to laugh). Guess orthopedic surgeons aren't familiar with the rule of thumb that says, "Measure twice, cut once". Just kidding, guys!

A third surgery was scheduled, but no more screws. A full hip replacement would be done this time. I have always heard that the third time is a charm; sure hope that holds true for hip surgeries. On a positive note, I will have to say that my surgeon was really quite a good seamster. Even after three surgeries, there only appeared to be one incision line on my leg. Good job!

To work or not to work…that was the question. Even though I had been given the green light to go back to work, I'll have to admit that I was just a little apprehensive. After all, it seemed that every time I stepped my foot through those office doors, one of my bones would break. Although I was still receiving the Aredia IV treatments and oral Fosamax had been added to help strengthen my bones, there was no definite evidence that it was working. I prayed that I would soon see some improvement and God answered my prayers.

My bone incidents occurred from May 1995 through August 1998, but listen up… days, weeks, months and even years passed with no more bone incidents. I had been able to work full time and actually was "movin' on up", the ladder that is, from transcriptionist to office manager/book-keeper. I loved the variety of work and being with my extended family -- Dr. Wilson, Dee, Jean, Jeanette, Lori and Scarlet. How I loved that bunch!

I wasn't the only one that was "movin' on up" -- our whole office staff was becoming a cutting edge, high-tech group! We had incorporated the electronic medical record and learned to e-prescribe, which was no easy task to set up. Even though we were busier than ever, we always had time for a laugh or two throughout the day. Dr. Wilson let us know that we were appreciated and took time to compliment us for a job well done. Many times he would say to us, "Best office in Lynchburg!"

What do you think made us the "best office in Lynchburg"? In my opinion, it was spending personal time with our patients and with each other. We took time to have lunch together out in the waiting room just to enjoy each other's company and talk and laugh. Then there were movie matinee "dates" with Dr. Wilson from time to time. He would choose the day, close the office for the afternoon, and take "his girls" out to lunch and a movie. And yes, he bought us a large popcorn and a large drink to share. I believe he liked the attention and remarks he got from the other moviegoers as he came strutting in the theater with six women. By the way, Dr. Wilson's wife, Sandra, knew about his "affair" with his "girls"

Several years passed and God blessed me with some good years of health and happiness. My bones grew stronger, I worked every day, was active in the choir, and various other church activities. I enjoyed spending time with my family, especially with Jacob and Justin, my two nephews. They brightened my life and gave me a reason to be active. I loved spoiling them and they spoiled me as well. They continually checked on me to see if I needed anything and were quick to respond if I called for them. They were and still are "my boys". *Proverbs 18:10 "The name of the Lord is a fortified tower; the righteous run to it and are safe."*

CHAPTER 10

The Big "C" Word

• • •

IN 2009, I NOTICED A small, rough spot on my right ankle. Since I didn't have any feeling in that foot, I thought I had probably just hit it on something and didn't realize it. I just put a little Neosporin Cream on it and kept going. After a week or so, the sore was still there and it didn't look any better. I was really concerned as to why this place wasn't healing, so I made an appointment with my Dermatologist. A biopsy was done and in a few days, I heard the big "C" word for the first time -- cancer. The spot turned out to be a squamous cell skin cancer. I was sent to UVA for Moh's surgery, the cancer was removed, the margins were clear all around the area, and I was good to go. Thank you, Jesus, for a simple surgery this time.

In August of 2010, the spot had returned in the same place. Another biopsy was done with another diagnosis of skin cancer. I assumed another Moh's surgery would be in order...WRONG!!! This time, I was sent to Dr. Henry Wilson, a Plastic Surgeon in Lynchburg. He was very thorough and put me through test after test in order to come up with the best options for me. I didn't see why he couldn't just cut out the affected area. But, Dr. H. Wilson said that would take away half of my foot and there was no assurance that it would heal.

After much research by Dr. H. Wilson, he wanted to try a new product on the market called Integra, which would cover the open wound and promote healing after the cancer was removed. In November of 2010, I had major surgery. Half of my ankle was removed and the Integra was put in place.

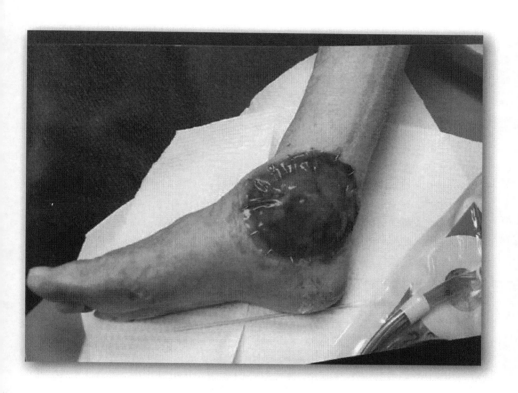

A Wound Vac was placed on my ankle to speed up the healing process and to keep fluid from gathering. I never thought I would look forward to crutches, but I was a happy camper when I was told I could be up and walking with them. Weekly visits to Dr. H. Wilson to keep check on the healing process became part of my normal routine.

I've heard it said that, "knowledge is power", so let me enlighten you a little about orthostatic hypotension so you will better understand where I'm coming from in future parts of my story. Medically, it is defined as a decrease in systolic blood pressure of 20 mm Hg or a decrease in diastolic blood pressure of 10 mm Hg within three minutes of standing when compared with blood pressure from the sitting or supine position. In other words, your blood pressure will drop when you go from lying to sitting and drop again as you go from sitting to standing. That was me!

After this particular surgery, I was really having a hard time staying upright due to my blood pressure and it was affecting my ability to do even the simplest tasks. My friend, Doc Lok, came to the rescue with a pill that would elevate my blood pressure and he told me to eat a lot of salt. I hear you...you're thinking, what a problem to have, since "normally" most folks are plagued by high blood pressure. I don't think the word "normal" has ever been associated with me as a patient. Rather, adjectives for me include "strange bird," "unique," "interesting," and of course, "weird," etc. Now that you have been enlightened, let's get back to work.

And that was exactly what I did; I went back to work...crutches, wound vac and all. The girls were constantly by my side to make sure I had everything I needed. Let me reiterate, they were much more than just my co-workers, they were my extended "family". Each one seemed to have their own special assignment to see that my needs were met. They were my "legs".

Front Row: Jeanette, Sharon and Scarlet
Back Row: Jean, Dee and Lori

The girls and I had just finished lunch and I headed to the bathroom. I usually locked the door behind me, but on this day I didn't, which turned out to be a blessing in disguise. Before I could get up from the commode, my blood pressure bottomed out and I had to start yelling for help (remember your lesson on orthostatic hypotension). Jean and Lori came running. At this point, just use your imagination as you try to picture them trying to get me off of the commode, get my pants pulled up, and lay me in the floor until my blood pressure came up, all while trying not to let me fall, put any weight on my foot, and not interfere with the Wound Vac. I'm sure that was quite a sight to behold and certainly not in their job description. Did you decide this was another God incident? I sure did!

The whole office was already stressed out because Dr. Wilson had decided to close his practice and I felt that I was adding additional stress to everyone. He had been practicing medicine in the field of Rheumatology since 1979. Most of our patients were Medicare age, so due to cuts in Medicare funding, government issues, and new regulations regarding the electronic medical record; it was just not feasible for him to keep the practice open. Although our hearts were saddened, we knew that he had made the right decision. After our initial crying spells, we tried to keep a positive attitude and a smile on our faces.

In the weeks to follow, each patient that came in was handed a letter informing them of the office closing. As some of them stood reading the letter, tears would start flowing and that would cause us to get teary eyed as well. It was so hard telling our patients goodbye. The last patients were seen around the middle of December so we could back up the files, get the servers out, and pack up all of the office belongings to be moved out of the building. *Isaiah 26:3 "You will keep in perfect peace those whose minds are steadfast, because they trust in you."*

CHAPTER 11

Tiny Bubbles

• • •

IT WAS NEARING CHRISTMAS AND all of us were looking forward to a few days off. It would be nice to celebrate the birth of Jesus and spend precious time with our families. I had been able to be up and about on my crutches, with no major blood pressure issues...that is until December 28th. On that day, my blood pressure dropped so low that I could not even sit up. I felt like I was going in and out of consciousness, so I was taken to the hospital and was admitted. I had a multitude of tests done to see if there might be some other underlying cause for my blood pressure problem, but all tests were negative and the diagnosis was still orthostatic hypotension. Doc Lok decided that this time he would use a "double barrel" approach to the problem and he added a second type of blood pressure medicine to the one I was already taking. It worked and I got to go home on New Year's Eve. To me, there's still no place like home!

Happy New Year, 2011! The office was officially closed and the whole staff was out of a job. Doesn't sound much like the beginning of a happy year, does it? Now, for the sixty-four-thousand-dollar question: What were we going to do? There was only one of us that would be able to re-tire. The rest would have to find a new job and that may not be an easy task at our age, not that we were ancient. Now, more than ever, we needed to trust in the Lord with all our hearts and lean not to our own under-standing. God would provide. And He did!

In time, each one found a new job...except me. Let me take that back... Dr. Wilson had lots of loose ends to tie up to finalize the office closing, so I began to work for him at home. He would bring the work to my house and come back to pick it up when I had finished. I was truly thankful for that opportunity because I still had a wound vac attached to my ankle and was still on crutches.

Dr. Wilson continued to bring more work to my house, but on one occasion, he was using a cane. Of course, I had to ask the normal question, "What in the world happened to you?" He told me that his hip had been bothering him for a while, and that soon he would have a total hip replacement.

Soon after this, I received a call from Scarlet and she was crying and asking me to please pray for her because she had just been diagnosed with breast cancer and would have to start chemotherapy soon. I cried with her and promised to pray for her.

Do you believe the superstition that things come in threes -- mainly bad things? Or, how about this one, "When it rains, it pours." I have never been a superstitious person because I believe that God is in control, but it really does seem as if three bad things often occur close together. #1 – Dr. Wilson's hip replacement, #2 – Scarlet diagnosed with breast cancer, and here comes #3 -- me. *Romans 12:12 "Rejoice in hope, be patient in tribulation, be constant in prayer."*

Now the time had come for me to see Dr. H. Wilson for another examination of my foot. After a thorough look at his "handiwork", he told me that I could put a little weight on it and walk again. Praise the Lord and Lord help me never to take any of your gifts for granted. A-men! My foot was still terribly swollen and I had to wear a little blue boot instead of a shoe, but that was no big deal...I could walk. Also, the new double-barrel blood pressure meds were still working and I was happy, happy, happy!

O.K. everybody, grab your ukuleles and let's sing along with Don Ho, "Tiny bubbles in the wine, make you feel happy, make you feel fine." But the tiny bubbles I had seen were not in any wine, nor did they make me feel happy or fine. The bubbles were scattered over my foot where the Integra had been applied. Just a little strange, I thought, even for me. So to be on the safe side, I made an appointment with Dr. H. Wilson to have them examined. He was honest and told me that he had never seen anything like that before and thought he should do a biopsy. He took several samples from random areas on my foot to send to the lab and then I was given a return appointment in which we would discuss the results. In my head, I think I knew that this was going to be bad news, but in my heart, I still had hope for different results. My head won instead of my heart -- the cancer had indeed returned for the third time.

Then, Dr. H. Wilson asked this question: "Has anyone ever checked your groin area?" Well, no. What a strange question since it was my foot that was the problem. However, there was a proper motive for the question. Dr. H. Wilson told me that if the cancer was aggressive, the next place it was likely to be found would be in the groin. Upon examination, he felt a couple of knots. I guess my next question seemed pretty dumb: "Do you think it is more cancer?" I will never forget his reply -- "If it looks like a duck, and quacks like a duck, then it usually is a duck." Well, isn't that just "ducky"? More biopsies with positive results of more cancer. But believe it or not, this was truly another "God incident". You will see why just a little later.

No time was wasted in scheduling the next progression of events. On May 2, 2011, I met with a general surgeon who discussed his operative plan with me, and the very next day, May 3, 2011, I was in surgery to remove the cancerous lymph nodes from my groin.

When the surgery was over and the surgeon met with my parents, the obvious first question was: "Were you able to remove all of the cancer?" "I did the best that I could", he replied, "but to answer your question -- no, I was not able to remove all of the cancer – your daughter has a very aggressive type of cancer." Then, he continued to explain that some of the lymph nodes had been invaded by the cancer to the point that they were fused together and also they were adjacent to a main artery. Trying to remove those would not have been in my best interest.

My parents thanked the surgeon and now they were faced with the unpleasant task of relaying to me what the surgeon had told them. Certainly, I had hoped for better news, but I knew that God would take care of me. In retrospect, don't you think that it was a little uncanny that Dr. H. Wilson decided to check the lymph nodes in my groin? If he had not done so… only God knows. Told you another "God incident", was coming, didn't I?

Since I had a very aggressive cancer, an aggressive plan of action needed to get under way. My surgeon suggested that I see a Radiation Oncologist as soon as possible.

Now I have faith in God, but I also have human weaknesses and I was scared!!! The next time I was able to go to church, I could not concentrate on the sermon. All I could think about was cancer. When it was time for the invitation, I went forward and asked my church congregation to pray for me. The minister asked me if I wanted to share my problem and that's when the tears started to flow. I only told him that I had a very serious health problem and just wanted prayer. I don't remember what was said after that, because the words of the song that the congregation was singing seemed to be magnified especially for me to hear: God will take care of you, through every day, o'er all the way; He will take care of you, God will take care of you. *Hebrews 11:1 "Now faith is the assurance of things hoped for, the conviction of things not seen."*

As suggested by my surgeon, I made an appointment to see Dr. Anita "Joy" Hilliard, Radiation Oncologist, at Pearson Cancer Center. She was in agreement that something needed to be done soon, but she also felt that I needed some additional time for my incision to heal. Dr. Hilliard also needed time to come up with a plan of action to make sure that the radiation beams did not come in contact with my transplanted kidney and pancreas. My situation was…not normal. Imagine that! My buddy, Doc Lok, called to tell me that he and Dr. Hilliard had a consultation and they would come up with the best plan possible for my situation. He also took time to pray for me. What a guy!

During the past week, so much emphasis had been placed on the cancer in my lymph nodes, but, hey guys, what about my foot? Bluntly and to the point, I was told that if I wanted to live, the foot would need to be amputated. Oops, sorry I asked that question. Although Doc Lok agreed, he still wanted another opinion.

So an appointment was made for me to see an orthopedic oncologist at MCV on May 10th. He had pretty much the same consensus that I would probably lose my foot, but he did offer one little ray of hope. He wanted me to see another Plastic Surgeon there who specialized in cases similar to mine. However, he was not working that day, so I would have to come back on May 12th, which just happened to be my birthday. Surely not my idea of how to spend my birthday, but if there was any chance my foot could be saved, it would be well worth it.

We traveled back to MCV on May 12th to see this new specialist I had been told about. I had mixed emotions that day, some of anxiety and some of hope. The surgeon came into my room and after a brief chat, he examined my foot and told me that there may be a possibility of saving it. Hallelujah! That was what I had been waiting to hear; tell me all about it. He began with, "There is a new method called Integra" ... that one word, "Integra", was all it took to burst my bubble of hope. Been there...done that and I told him about my experience with Integra.

Since my appointment had been made on the spur of the moment, I knew he did not have a chance to review my records and find out that Integra had already been tried and failed, but now that he knew, he joined the rest of the group that felt amputation was my only option. Happy Birthday to me!

At this point, seven specialists had told me that my foot needed to be amputated for me to live. That was really a hard pill to swallow. I just couldn't imagine what it would be like without my foot. *Matthew 21:21 And Jesus answered them, "Truly, I say to you, if you have faith and do not doubt, you will not only do what has been done to the fig tree, but even if you say to this mountain, 'Be taken up and thrown into the sea,' it will happen."*

CHAPTER 12

Going, Going, Gone

• • •

DISAPPOINTMENTS COME TO EVERYONE, BUT the world keeps turning and
life goes on. So, on Saturday, May 14th, all of the office girls got together
at Charley's for a birthday celebration for Scarlet and me. I was even able
to push the events of the previous week to the back of my mind for a brief
time.

It had been a good day, but that night was a different story. I was cold
when I went to bed, but that's nothing too unusual for me, so I just put
a sweatshirt on over my night shirt and cranked up the electric blanket,
but I still couldn't get warm. In a very short time, I was burning up and
throwing up. Mama immediately called 911 and as we were waiting for
the rescue squad, I started saying my goodbyes to each member of my
family and told them how much I loved them. I felt so strange that I honestly thought I was going to die.

As the ambulance was traveling to the Emergency Room, I overheard
the EMT say they were in transit with a forty-seven-year-old female with
possible sepsis, which can be a potentially life-threatening complication of
an infection. Once at the ER, after lots of blood work, it was determined
that I did not have sepsis, but rather an infection in my groin where the
lymph nodes had been removed. I was hospitalized and treated with IV
antibiotics.

The next day, my surgeon came by and told me the infection was due
to fluid trapped under the incision and it would have to be opened up in

order to drain. Dumb me, I thought they would take me to the O.R., put me to sleep, and probably insert a drain tube. Oh, how wrong I was. The surgeon took a small sterile scalpel and right then and there in my hospital bed, he cut that sucker open and blood and fluid spurted out like a volcano. It's for sure no fluid will get trapped there any longer, because now there was a gaping hole in my leg.

On a more positive note, the IV antibiotics were doing their job and the site was healing once again. I felt super good and was looking forward to going home in a few days. Oh, was I ever so wrong!

Now enters Doc Lok. Even when he wasn't assigned to my case, if he knew I was hospitalized, he would always drop by to see me. I was really glad to see him and we had a nice conversation -- up to a point. Now, just listen to this scenario: In his "as a matter of fact" voice, he said that we might as well go ahead with the amputation since I was already there. Do what? That was certainly not what I was expecting to hear from "my buddy" -- the one who would usually help me to escape from this place a little sooner than I would be scheduled for discharge. Now he wants me to stay here so they can cut off my foot. "Doc Lok, I just want to go home, even if it's for just one night. I want to take a shower and then walk around my house on BOTH feet just one more time." I know it must have broken his heart to have to tell me that I couldn't do that because of hospital regulations. *Romans 8:28 "And we know that in all things God works for the good of those who love him, who have been called according to his purpose."* Lord, I'm trying hard to understand how I can find any "good" in having my foot amputated.

While trying to be worked into the operating room schedule, it was... wait for this, wait for that...wait, wait, wait. I could have been home and back while I was doing all of that waiting. Dr. Eschenroeder would be doing my amputation and he dropped by to see me before he went home. Our conversation started with the normal chit-chat, but it didn't take but a few minutes until he was trying to convince me that this surgery was actually going to be good for me. He reminded me that I had been dragging that "old diseased foot" around for years and later on down the road,

I would be glad that it was gone. Yeah, right! That was MY foot he was talking about, MY foot that he was going to cut off and there he was trying to convince me that I would be glad when it was gone. I'm not buying that!!!

My D-Day had arrived, May 18, 2011 -- a day that will live in infamy. Oops, that's the wrong D-Day, or was it?   Surgery was scheduled for noon, but since I was a "work-in", no guarantee could be made as to exactly what time they would get around to me. Lord, I know Your Word tells me "do not be anxious about anything". I'm not anxious, Lord, I am flat out scared! Please help me through this, A-men.

As noon approached, my room and the hallway outside of my room was filled with a huge support team -- my family, co-workers, neighbors, and many church members. Lots of hugs and prayers mingled with tears. What an outpouring of love! Simply overwhelming!

Noon had come and gone, as well as one o'clock, two o'clock, three, and four. Mama and I walked up and down the hall what seemed like a hundred times as Daddy talked with our many friends. I knew that this would be the last day that I would ever walk on my own two feet. I couldn't seem to get that thought out of my mind, so I wanted to just walk, walk, walk.

Around five o'clock, an orderly finally arrived to take me down for surgery. I couldn't hold back the tears and neither could my family and friends. I will always remember those who were there for me and my family that day.

It wasn't a lengthy surgery. I would call it a 1, 2, 3 surgery -- 1. Cut the foot off. 2. Stitch up the stump. 3. Bandage it up. Actually, my foot plus eleven inches of my leg was amputated. Then, it was off to the recovery room for a brief period and then back to my own room where my family was waiting for me. I was feeling pretty good...note I said WAS, because in a matter of a few minutes, I was throwing up everywhere. I had been given Lortab while I was in the recovery room. No one had given me the opportunity to tell them that I don't do Lortab! Finally, my stomach settled down and I slept like a baby.

Mama stayed with me through the night -- that's just what mama's do. She was a little afraid that I might wake up groggy and try to get out of bed, forgetting that now I only had one foot.

The next day, it was business as usual. I was amazed at how good I felt. I ate breakfast, got washed up, then the physical therapists came in to teach me how to use a walker. Off we went for a walk, rather a hop, down the hallway. They were surprised to see how well I could maneuver with that walker. I informed them of the many times I had used crutches and/or a walker due to my previous surgeries on my feet and legs. It was decided right then and there that I did not need their services.

Representatives from various other agencies were in and out of my room all day checking to see what durable medical equipment I already had, such as a wheelchair, shower seat, bedside commode, etc., and what I would need. They wanted to get it ordered and have it sent to my home so it would be waiting for me when I got there. So many caring people... so grateful!

It had been a very busy day and I was tired. I got back into bed to rest for a while and soon my foot started to itch. "Mama, will you scratch my foot for me, it's itching?" Mama proceeded to scratch the only foot I had left. "No, my right foot." Now she knew that I didn't have a right foot any longer, but she went along with my request and made scratching motions where my right foot had been. I guess she thought I was hallucinating, but it really felt like my foot was still there.

The sensation I was feeling is called phantom limb -- the term given to any sensory phenomenon (except pain) which is felt at an absent limb or a portion of the limb. Phantom pain refers to the feeling of pain in an absent limb or a portion of a limb. The pain sensation varies from individual to individual.

Dr. Eschenroeder came in to see me on Friday morning to check my "stump" (the distal end of a limb left after amputation). He gave himself a pat on the back for the good job he had done and I had to agree with him, as I swallowed a mouthful of "crow". Then came music to my ears -- you can go home. I love you, Dr. "E".

Did I luck out with all of these wonderful doctors or what? Luck played no part, but the "or what" certainly did – another "God incident". My Heavenly Father had all of my doctors on standby long before I ever met any of them! What an awesome God we serve! *Psalm 16:8 "I keep my eyes always on the Lord. With him at my right hand, I will not be shaken."*

CHAPTER 13

Simply Radiating

• • •

THERE IT IS -- MY Home Sweet Home! I am one happy camper. I had to make a few adjustments here and there, but nothing major. I preferred crutches over a walker and used them most of the time. Whenever I needed to go up or down the stairs, I would just sit on my butt and give myself a push up step after step until I had conquered all fourteen of them. Yes, I said fourteen. Our home is a tri-level and there are five steps from the first to the second level, and nine steps from the second to the third level.

Often times, even when I wasn't on the steps, I would find myself scooting from room to room on my butt. It was just easier than fooling with crutches or a walker. Man, just look at these muscles in my arms. One might think I had been lifting weights. In a manner of speaking, I had been lifting weight -- my own.

My stay at home was short lived. My blood pressure was acting up again and I couldn't even sit up without feeling like I was going to pass out. What's more, it was getting harder to breathe and my heart rate had dropped to thirty-eight. No time was wasted calling 911. When the rescue squad arrived, they checked my vital signs, quickly loaded me into the vehicle, and off we went speeding up the road with sirens blaring to let everyone in our pathway know that the patient being transported (that was me) was in serious condition. As if that wasn't enough, the EMT placed defibrillator paddles on my back – just in case, as he put it.

When we reached the hospital, I was ushered into a bay with a room full of nurses and technicians waiting for me. It was like something right out of a movie -- my shirt was ripped off and orders were being yelled out from one to another to do "this" and then do "that". I didn't know what was wrong with me, but from all indications… it was not good. I was so frightened.

Daddy had followed the rescue squad and was in my room during all of the commotion. He was not going to let me out of his sight. Mama had planned to come a little later, but when she heard the sirens start up as the rescue squad left the house, she dropped everything and headed for the hospital. She was so afraid that by the time she got there, I would not be alive.

When all of my tests were finally evaluated, the results showed that I had a heart block. However, it could easily be remedied with a pacemaker. Glory, glory, hallelujah! I was actually looking forward to this procedure. However,… I still don't like that word…it happened to be Memorial Day weekend, which means it was a holiday, which means some doctors were on vacation, which means no surgeries would be scheduled until Tuesday, except in the event of an emergency, which inevitably means I would have to wait until at least Tuesday before I could get my pacemaker, which means my home away from home would be in the Coronary Care Unit until then. Did you get all of that?

Tuesday finally arrived, but it was almost 5:00 P.M. before my procedure was done. I was totally shocked when I was told that I could go home around 7:00 P.M. It was music to my ears, but Mama certainly wasn't hearing the same music. After all, it had only been two hours since the pacemaker had been implanted in her little girl's chest and her brain went into high gear thinking of "what ifs" that could happen when I got home. She was more than a little anxious to say the least.

Mama was sitting in a chair while I was being discharged and one of the nurses looked at her and asked if she was all right. When she didn't respond, the nurse started checking her blood pressure, and heart rate and in a matter of minutes, she was in a wheelchair being transported downstairs to the Emergency Room.

Now, wait a minute, I thought I was the patient. Well, it wasn't me anymore, I had been discharged. To make a long story short, Mama had a severe panic attack, but was home in a couple of hours. I wonder if I could have had anything to do with her anxiety -- no way, it couldn't have been me! Sorry, Mama.

O.K. Let's have a brief recap of events: May 3rd – lymph nodes were removed from my groin, May 18th – my leg was amputated below the knee, and now on May 31st -- I received one of the newest pacemakers on the market which was MRI compatible.

It turned out to be another "God Incident" as you will later see. *Psalm 34:19 "The righteous person may have many troubles, but the LORD delivers him from them all."*

Life was good. Things were starting to get back to normal, but one day, Mama told me she had a problem. Now believe me, I didn't want Mama to end up in the E.R. again with another panic attack, so I asked her what was wrong. She told me that whenever I went up or down the stairs on my butt, I would always stay right in the middle of the treads. She wanted me to start sliding from side to side so I would keep the whole stair tread dusted. That way, she wouldn't have to vacuum them. Mama, sometimes I wonder about you!

May had been a chaotic month to say the least, but the month of June was starting off in my favor. I was healing from all of my procedures and enjoying being at home with my family. But, take a moment to rewind and remember that I still needed to have radiation treatments. Dr. Hilliard had been working for weeks to come up with a plan to radiate my groin area and now, everything seemed to be in order and we had a "go".

On July 1, 2011, we started our daily treks back and forth to the Cancer Center as I began a series of thirty treatments. By WE, I mean Mama, Daddy, and me. We had dubbed ourselves "The Traveling Trio" because where you would see one, the other two would be close behind. My Mama and Daddy were the world's best support team, but God brought so many new people into my life during this time who supported me as well. Dr. Hilliard and the radiation technicians quickly became my friends. They were such kind and compassionate people -- simply radiating! Did you get that? *Psalm 119:105 Your word is a lamp for my feet, a light on my path.*

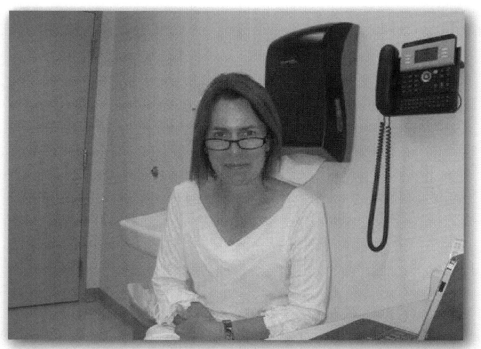

Dr. Anita "Joy" Hilliard

Not only was I receiving my radiation treatments, I also had a physical therapist that was coming to my house to help me with exercises that would strengthen my stump in preparation for a prosthesis. Then came my initial visit to the prosthetic office. I was given shrinker socks to wear, which would mold my stump into the proper shape for a prosthetic leg. Did you hear that -- I'm going to get a new leg! Once again, I had more new friends to add to my growing list. These had been busy, busy, but productive days for me.

We had traveled back and forth to the Langhorne Road area so many times in the past weeks, that Mama commented we could probably get in the van and put it on auto pilot and it would take us there. Not a good idea, Mama. Just keep your hands on the wheel, Daddy.

We were off to the prosthetic office to design my new leg. First, a plaster mold of my stump would be made, and then a fiberglass socket would be formed which would attach to a foot. By the way, what kind of foot would you like? Do you want a space between your big toe and second toe so you can wear flip-flops? You've got to be kidding, but they weren't. The type of foot really didn't matter to me. I just wanted to walk again.

That day came sooner than I expected and I can't begin to explain the array of emotions I was feeling as we were driving to the prosthetic office. When we arrived, I was taken to a room and in came my prosthetist with my new leg -- MY NEW LEG!

My stump was placed into the prosthesis and "just look at me, everybody." There I was, standing on two feet. It didn't matter that one of them was plastic. I was even able to take a few steps. So amazing! I looked at Mama and tears were running down her cheeks; happy tears for a change. Since this was only a check socket for proper measurements, I couldn't take it home. I would have to wait a little longer for a permanent one to be built.

On July 13, 2011, I got a call to let me know that my permanent leg was ready for pick-up. Sounded like a catalog order -- your order is ready for pick-up at register three.

When I got to the office that day, everyone there was as excited as I was. They were all standing around watching as I put my leg on, stood up, and took a few wobbly steps. A few tears were even shed by some of the staff. What a wonderful miracle. God is so good. I'm going to be okay.

When I got home, I just wanted to walk and walk and walk. I had to use my walker for balance at first. Then I moved to a cane for a brief period and then with a few words of encouragement for myself -- "You can do this, girl", I let go and just walked. Hey everybody, look, I'm walking. I got a standing ovation from my family. I was so thankful.

Isaiah 40:31 "But those who hope in the LORD will renew their strength. They will soar on wings like eagles; they will run and not grow weary, they will walk and not be faint."

"They will walk...they will walk...they will walk." What words of encouragement!

My physical therapist was scheduled to come back soon with his objective being to teach me how to use my walker and cane to maneuver about on my prosthetic leg. Boy, did I have a surprise for him. When the doorbell rang, I walked to the door unassisted, and just smiled at him as he stood there with his mouth hanging open. Then he said, "You're discharged!" He did come in for a while and watched me walk all around the house. He was amazed and told me that he had never had a patient that had progressed so quickly. Then, he really did discharge me. I wanted to get out and go places now that I could walk and the "traveling trio" did just that.

. *Philippians 4:13 "I can do all things through Christ who gives me strength."*

CHAPTER 14

Six Weeks or Six Months?

• • •

ABOUT A MONTH HAD PASSED and my prosthesis was hurting my leg behind the knee. I thought an adjustment might need to be made. As I removed my prosthesis, I felt a knot behind my knee and so did my prosthetist. We both had the same opinion -- probably just a Baker's cyst. However, (I wish that word would quit popping up) the pain behind my knee was getting worse, making it difficult for me to walk.

I made an appointment with my buddy, Dr. Eschenroeder. He did some x-rays at his office, but wasn't completely satisfied, so he gave me orders for some additional tests at the Radiology Department. Now, you have to remember that I worked in a doctor's office for twenty-five years, so when I read the orders for a biopsy of the knot behind my knee plus x-rays of my knee, hip and chest; it didn't take a rocket scientist to know that there was more to this than just checking for a Baker's Cyst. It would be several days before someone would be getting back to me with the test results.

However, it wasn't Dr. Eschenroeder that called with the test results; it was Doc Lok. He wanted to set up an after-hours appointment to meet with me and my parents to review the results. An after-hours appointment is never a good sign, especially when your parents have been requested to come as well. I was terrified.

On September 30, 2011, we met with Doc Lok at 5:00 P.M. My nurse came in to check my vitals and as she was walking out of the door, she commented, "no matter what, you are going to be just fine." Gee, thanks for those words of encouragement. It was obvious that she already knew something that I didn't and that scared me even more.

In a few minutes, Doc Lok came into the room, but he was not smiling or joking around as he usually did. He got right to the point and told us that the knot behind my knee was not a Baker's Cyst, but more cancer. I had tried to prepare myself for that news, but never in a million years would I have been able to prepare myself for what was to come -- the cancer had also moved to my lungs. Of course, none of us could hold back the tears. Doc Lok told us that he also couldn't hold back the tears when he first read the report. I was so completely caught off guard that I didn't know what to say or even what to think -- just totally in shock!

Doc Lok had always been at the top of my support team and he had always been able to come up with a solution for my problems, but not this time. He just gave me a big hug and reminded me, as he always had in the past, that God was in control.

We sometimes have to experience disappointment for us to have a story to tell. The power to heal from our disappointment equips us with the strength to rise up again and move beyond it all. We not only become stronger, but wise enough to recognize and handle disappointment in the future.

The next order of business would be to find a good Oncologist. Doc Lok recommended Dr. Kathleen Paul and that was good enough for me. Our first meeting with her was on October 4, 2011. I could tell from the minute I met her that it was no coincidence that Doc Lok had recommended her. Quiz time -- if it isn't a coincidence, then what is it? You got it -- a "God incident".

In a very soft spoken, but direct manner, she told me that my cancer was very rare and very aggressive and there was no known cure at the present time. I was certain that she had just given me my death sentence. Now, I consider myself to be a strong person and I had been trying hard to keep my composure, but this was more than I could handle and I couldn't hold back my tears any longer. Neither could Mama and Daddy.

Dr. Paul gave us time to regain our composure and then she continued, "However, there are several types of chemo we can try that might slow down the progression of the cancer. In my past experiences, the word, however, had always seemed to be followed by bad news. But this "however" at least brought with it a small glimmer of hope. Then, I just had to ask, "How long do you think I have? Six weeks, six months?" I will never forget her answer..." I just don't know; I hope so." Now that was enough to make even the strongest person want to find a rock and crawl under it. But I had never been a quitter and I wasn't about to begin now. I wanted to fight for my life even if it was for only a few weeks or months. Chemo treatments would be started as soon as possible.

That night, I couldn't sleep. The events of the day kept spinning around and around in my head and I was actually planning my funeral. The next day when I told Mama and Daddy who I wanted as pall bearers, Mama gave me "that look" which usually meant a lecture was forthcoming. But that was not the case. Instead, we just reasoned together. Did Dr. Paul actually know how much time I had left? No, only God alone knew that. Would putting everything in God's hands be the solution? Of course!

Then and there we made a pact that no matter what we had to face in the future, we would look for something positive in each day. From that day until this, our family starts the day with our paraphrased version of *Psalm 118:24* -- *"This is the day the Lord has made; I will rejoice and be glad in it."*

October 7, 2011, was the day for my first chemo treatment. Dr. Paul had chosen to try an IV treatment called Erbitux and it would not cause me to lose my hair. Now, that was unexpected news. HOWEVER, (here we go again) the drug did have a tendency to cause allergic reactions, usually with the first or second dose. I was quite anxious as the IV drip was started and within minutes, boy, did I ever react. Dr. Paul was called immediately and the crash cart was brought into my room to be on standby. I had severe pain in my back, low blood pressure, nausea, vomiting and later a skin rash. Still, Dr. Paul didn't think this was an allergic reaction to the

Erbitux, but rather my body reacting to the harsh chemo drugs. I would just have to trust her on this one...and I did.

She decided to stop the treatment for about thirty minutes and then try it again. I was quite anxious when the drip was restarted, but Dr. Paul remained in my room for a while to make sure all would go well and it did. I'll have to admit that as the time for my second treatment approached, I was a little on edge, but there were no problems -- praise the Lord. I had minimal side effects from the Erbitux, mostly nausea, vomiting, and fatigue.

Our game plan was for me to have six treatments followed by a CT scan that would let us know if the Erbitux was having any effect on the tumors. Part one of the game plan had been completed and I was ready to start the second phase.

I arrived at the Cancer Center for treatment seven, was taken to my room and was waiting for my nurse to come back with my pre-treatment meds. Instead of my nurse, Dr. Paul came in and announced that I would not be having a treatment that day -- the Erbitux was not working. In fact, the tumors in my lungs had actually grown. What a letdown! I tried my best to hold back the tears, but I couldn't. I had had such high hopes.

What now? Dr. Paul was already way ahead of the game because she had Plan B already in the works. She wanted me to begin taking an oral chemo drug called Xeloda. Why not...what did I have to lose... except possibly my hair?

As we left the Cancer Center that day, Mama wanted to try to lift my spirits, if possible, so we headed for the mall. I'm not sure I remember much about our shopping trip that day, but I know Mama had good intentions. Daddy was at home waiting for us and when we told him the news, he just put the three of us in a big group hug and held us tight. And yes, real men do cry!

A week had gone by and it was time to start the Xeloda; two pills in the morning and three at night for two weeks, skip a week, and start all over again. They made me so sick that I threw up morning and night and at times, throughout the day as well. My daily routine turned out to be: Take pills and puke, then take more pills and puke again. I was so tired and weak that I found myself taking afternoon naps; something I had never done before in my life. I took the Xeloda until February and then it was time for more scans.

As sick as I had been, I thought that stuff had surely been working. WRONG! Same bad news – no effect on the tumors; they were still growing. No need for tears, just more prayers. Don't get me wrong; there is nothing wrong with crying. It is not a sign of weakness, but rather just a human reaction in times of great sorrow and trials and also in times of joy and happiness. If you remember, *"Jesus wept." John 11:35*

There was one more chemo drug left to try and this one would make my hair fall out. Who needs hair as long as there was a chance that the tumors would shrink? Let's get this show on the road. But, Dr. Paul thought my body needed a break from chemo drugs, so we would wait two weeks before round three. *Psalm 121:1-2 "I lift up my eyes to the mountains -- where does my help come from? My help comes from the LORD, the Maker of heaven and earth."*

During that waiting period, there were places to go and people to see. I had an appointment with Dr. Soni Carlton, Dermatologist, and since my prosthesis was still hurting my leg, I went in my wheelchair. A thorough exam was done and only one actinic keratosis (a rough, scaly patch on your skin that develops from years of exposure to the sun) was found. I usually had at least a half dozen that had to be frozen. The chemo had done a number on my skin; too bad it couldn't have been my lungs.

Dr. Carlton finished up my exam and was leaving the room just as I was moving from the exam chair to my wheelchair and... I fell. She asked if she could try to help me up, but I declined; I just wanted to sit there. I know she felt horrible, but there was nothing she could have done to prevent it.

Mama was in the waiting room and I asked one of the nurses to get her. She tried to help me up, but moving my leg the least bit caused excruciating pain. I knew it was broken -- and it was my good leg! I was taken by ambulance to the hospital and x-rays were done confirming that my femur was indeed broken. Surgery was scheduled for the next day, February 9, 2012. A plate and screws were attached to the femur from just below the hip replacement all the way down to my knee. Doctor's orders were to keep my leg out straight, elevated, and absolutely no weight bearing. Talk about not having a leg to stand on. To this day, I still have not figured out what caused me to fall and Mama still wonders if she could have kept me from falling if she had been there with me. No need dwelling on the past.

As a reminder, there are fourteen steps from our entrance foyer to my bedroom. Before my accident, I was able to sit on my butt and scoot myself up the steps using my "good" leg to push with. Well, that was history, so I had to take up residence in the spare bedroom downstairs. I'm a creature of habit and I don't like change and I didn't like sleeping downstairs. But, you gotta do what you gotta do! Mama slept on the sofa in the family room so she would be close to me in case I needed help during the night. I could tell already that it was going to be a long eight weeks.

Oops, I just had a thought...Hey, Mama, I've got to go for a chemo treatment on February 27th. How do you and Daddy plan to get me there? Good question. I couldn't sit in the seats in the van because I had to keep my leg out straight. The truck bed might have been an option in warm weather, but it was February. Here's an idea, let's take the center bench seat out of the van and go from there. So Daddy took the seat out and Mama put quilts and pillows on the floorboard for me to sit on. There is no way to explain the way I was moved in and out of the van, while trying to keep my leg in a stable position. I just wish that someone could have recorded it for America's Funniest Home Videos.

It was time to put Plan C into action -- a third attempt to slow down the progression of the tumors in my lungs. Taxol and Carboplatin were the drugs of choice. The Taxol was a three-hour drip and the Carboplatin only took thirty minutes. Blood work and pre-meds were done before each treatment, making the total time around five hours. They would be administered every three weeks. I chose Monday as my treatment day with the thought that if I got sick from the chemo, maybe I would feel well enough by the next Sunday to go to church. Attending church was, and still is, a major part of my life. Monday arrived and it was time for treatment #1 – no adverse effects during the drip, but afterwards, sick, sick, sick -- nausea, vomiting, low blood pressure, fatigue, and no appetite. *Psalm 34:4 "I sought the Lord and he heard me; and delivered me from all my fears."*

CHAPTER 15

"Hair" Today, Gone Tomorrow

• • •

DURING THE THREE-WEEK INTERVAL BEFORE my next treatment, I began to have difficulty breathing. The tumors were growing and my lungs were filling with fluid. I couldn't lay down without feeling like I was choking. A hospital bed was ordered with the hope that I would be able to adjust the head of the bed to a sitting position in order to breathe better.

Dr. Paul arranged for me to be seen by a Pulmonologist (a physician who possesses specialized knowledge and skill in the diagnosis and treatment of lung conditions and diseases). Visits to his office were routine: Chest x-rays were done to determine the amount of fluid in my lungs, then a needle attached to a large syringe was poked in my back to draw off the fluid. After several visits, the doctor thought it would be to my advantage to insert a catheter that would continually drain the fluid so he wouldn't have to keep poking holes in my back. The procedure was planned for my next visit.

The time arrived for The Traveling Trio to head for my next appointment; x-rays first, then the procedure we had discussed. Soon, the doctor came into my room with a somewhat puzzled look on his face. As you can well imagine, my thought was that more bad news was on the way. Now listen carefully to this: The doctor said, "I don't understand it, but your x-rays show that there is very little fluid in your lungs, so we won't need to do anything for you today." Mama and I chimed in almost simultaneously -- WE DO! It was a miracle from God!

I was told that no further appointments would be necessary unless my symptoms reoccurred. Daddy had been waiting for us and when we told him the good news, we had a celebration right then and there in the waiting room. Smiles, smiles, and more smiles. Thank you, Jesus. On the way home, Mama serenaded Daddy and me with the Hallelujah Chorus.

It was not quite time for my second treatment; maybe two and a half weeks had passed. Mama had just washed my hair and as I was combing it, something caught between my fingers. I looked at my hands; they were full of hair -- my hair. It was coming out by the handful. I knew it was going to happen sooner or later, but I didn't think it would be this soon. After all, I had only had one treatment. My head looked like a checkerboard, a bald spot in one place and spot with hair in another. I tried combing what hair I had left over the bald spots, but the more I combed, the more my hair fell out.

After about three days, I asked Mama to get the clippers and buzz the rest of it off. As I looked in the mirror, the reflection was not what I was used to seeing – there was some bald person staring back at me! I didn't know whether to laugh or cry, so I tried giving myself some words of consolation: It will grow back, it will grow back, it will grow back.

Ready, set, go...for treatment #2. Mama and Daddy loaded me into my special floorboard seat in the van and off we went. My treatment went smoothly, but in the next few days, the side effects of the chemo kicked in and this time I didn't just vomit -- I puked. What's the difference you might ask? By my definition, vomit comes up in quarts, but "puke" comes in gallons. Gross!

F.Y.I. – Not only was my head totally bald, but every piece of hair on my entire body had fallen out, even my eyebrows and eyelashes. I had to constantly remember my words of consolation, "*...and it came to pass.*"

Dr. Paul wanted to schedule a CT scan before I had a third treatment to see if this chemo was having any effect on the tumors. The scan was done and we went to see her on April 11, 2012 to review the results. She walked into my room with THE paper in her hand, and her expression seemed to be a bit on the serious side. My heart started to pound because my previous scans had brought nothing but bad news.

Dr. Paul rolled her chair over beside me so we could look at the report together. But first she made what I thought to be a strange remark; she commented that she had to look at my name and date of birth twice to make sure that these were actually my scans. Then, she began to read the results: The 7 cm nodule in your lung is down to 1.5 cm "Near Complete Resolution." Let me say those words one more time -- NEAR COMPLETE RESOLUTION. "Thank you, Jesus" was my first response and Mama's and Daddy's as well. Then, lots of smiles and hugs and tears of joy. Oh, what a happy day! ANOTHER MIRACLE FROM GOD! The evidence of His mercy, grace, and power. *Psalm 119:71 "It was good for me to be afflicted so that I might learn your decrees."*

My final chemo treatment was on June 18, 2012 and scans were repeated on July 9, 2012. The results: NED, no evidence of disease. There was no fluid in the lungs at all. CT scans have been done of my lungs every three to six months since that grand and glorious day, April 11, 2012, and praise God, with the same miraculous results each time – NO EVIDENCE OF DISEASE. The best words a cancer patient could ever hear! By the way, by this time, my femur had healed and I was able to walk again.

Note: I am living proof that God still performs miracles, but they are not at the direction or discretion of believers, but a decision of God alone. Why does God miraculously heal some while choosing not to heal others? I don't know! In God's higher wisdom, He knows who to heal and what is best for the believer when He chooses not to heal. Our sufferings and afflictions serve to work out a purpose that we may not be able to understand at this time (Romans 8). No matter what, don't give up, keep trusting in God and keep praying.

Dr. Kathleen Paul and me

CHAPTER 16
Lucky Thirteen

• • •

ALMOST THIRTEEN MONTHS HAD PASSED. Thirteen months free from broken bones, chemo, and its side effects. Thirteen months to enjoy family activities and attend church and choir practice on a regular basis, and thirteen months to grow hair which incidentally came back curly. I had never had curls before. I had been blessed! But as Paul Harvey would say, now here's the rest of the story:

In August of 2013, my right upper leg was very painful. The thought that it might be more cancer had not entered my mind, because I had been told that cancer usually doesn't hurt. Probably just pulled a muscle. When the pain continued, I began to be somewhat concerned, so I made an appointment with Dr. Paul.

When she examined my leg, she felt a knot and immediately scheduled me for an MRI. No smiles or hallelujahs with these results; there were two nodules in my upper leg and they were positioned right on top of a nerve, which was causing the pain. Note: This was the first MRI that had been scheduled since I had received my pacemaker in May of 2011. As you may recall in an earlier chapter, I told you that the pacemaker I received was MRI compatible which I believed to be a "God incident" and the reason would be forthcoming. Well, here it comes: Had I not received that special type of pacemaker, an MRI would no longer have been an option for me.

Unlike CT scans, which use X-rays, MRI scans use powerful magnetic fields and radio frequency pulses to produce detailed pictures of organs, soft tissues, bone and other internal body structures. Differences between normal and abnormal tissue is often clearer on an MRI image than a CT. Just what I needed. Thank you, Lord.

What now, Dr. Paul? She decided we would repeat the same regimen of Taxol and Carboplatin that we used before since it did so well. I won't go into a lot of detail, because this experience was a carbon copy of the last one -- have the treatment, then would come the nausea, puking and fatigue and a wave goodbye to the hair once again. But, God with His never ending mercy and grace, showered His blessings upon me and both tumors disappeared. Soon I was able to return to my normal activities -- even driving. And...my hair grew back and it was curly this time as well. God is good!

It was now September 2014. Another thirteen months had passed. Hey, what's with this number thirteen? Even though I had never been superstitious, I was beginning to wonder if there really could be some kind of connection between number thirteen (13) and bad luck.

The pain in my leg was back in the same general area, but more intense. I am not a "pill-popper" by nature, but Tylenol and an occasional Tramadol would soon become my close companions until I could get an appointment with Dr. Paul. Once again, an MRI was done and again another confirmation of cancer. Isn't the third time for the same type of incident supposed to be a charm? We'll see.

Round three of chemo would be a repeat of round two -- same chemo drugs (Taxol and Carboplatin), same time frame (every three weeks). Treatment number one was picture perfect. Treatment number two was started with my three-hour drip of Taxol -- no problems. Next came the thirty-minute drip of Carboplatin.

After about ten minutes, I began to feel very nauseated. I asked Mama to get the trash can for me because I felt like I had to throw up. My nurse just happened to be close enough to hear me ask for a trash can and came into my room to see if I was having a problem. Now, do you really think that was a coincidence? No way! Another "God incident". One look at me was all it took for her to know I was having an allergic reaction and headed into anaphylactic shock.

A call went out to Dr. Paul and an emergency response team to come with a crash cart. An Epi-pen was jabbed into my leg and Dr. Paul monitored my heart and blood pressure while the rest of the team went about their assigned tasks. Several bags of fluids rolled through my veins, but it took quite a while before my blood pressure was up enough to allow me to sit up. What just happened?

Dr. Paul explained to me that Carboplatin had a track record for causing allergic reactions after a number of treatments and now it would have to be added to my list of drug related allergies. I still had four more treatments scheduled and they would be continued using the Taxol only.

On December 31, 2014, I went to the Cancer Center for my sixth and final treatment. After checking my blood work, Dr. Paul came into my room and told me everything was good to go. However,...it's been awhile, but I'm compelled to use that word again. The day before, I had noticed some little blisters on my skin in the bend of my leg. Since Dr. Paul was already in my room, I thought it would be a good idea to let her take a look at them. She examined them and proceeded to tell my nurse that I would not be having a treatment that day. Instead, I would be going for another MRI. The results once again confirmed more cancer. It was evident that the Taxol alone was not working.

If I remember correctly, I believe Dr. Paul told me that there were three chemo options for me; all of which had been tried. Realizing this, I was full of questions: Where do we go from here? What's next? Have we run out of options?

Previously, genetic mutation testing had been done and Dr. Paul told me there was one other chemo drug that matched my genetic profile, but it had not been approved for internal squamous cell cancer, and it was VERY expensive. That seemed to be of no consequence to her; she would be on a mission to try to get the insurance company to give their approval anyway. First, she wrote a letter explaining my situation and asked for approval for me to try the new drug. The answer -- NO! Next, she wrote an appeal letter. The answer -- NO! Then, I wrote an appeal letter. The answer -- NO! Three strikes and you're out.

My next appointment with Dr. Paul was for a "what do we do next" consultation. I knew there were no more chemo options and I wondered if I had any options at all. It was at that point she told me that in her opinion, the only way to save my life was to have my leg amputated at the hip. A-M-P-U-T-A-T-E-D. I certainly had not considered that as an option and I just sat there a bit dumbfounded, trying to take in what I had just heard. She relayed to me that she knew she was thinking "outside of the box", but her thought was that if the leg was removed, there was a chance that all of the cancer would be removed along with it. If I should decide to go with this option, surgery would need to be done as soon as possible or the cancer may spread beyond the leg. In my mind, I knew that what she had said made perfect sense, but my heart just wasn't on the same page. Before making a decision this drastic, she wanted me to get a second opinion from an Orthopedic/Oncology surgeon at MCV. Amputated -- cut the rest of my leg off... It doesn't take a rocket scientist to know that I was between a rock and a hard place. *Psalm 46:1-3 "God is our refuge and strength, an every-present help in trouble. Therefore, we will not fear, though the earth give way and the mountains fall into the heart of the sea, though its waters roar and foam and the mountains quake with their surging."*

CHAPTER 17

Not a Leg to Stand on

• • •

So, OFF TO MCV WE went, the Traveling Trio, in action again – Daddy, Mama and me. We met with Dr. Gregory Domson. He was very nice, very thorough, and I might add a handsome hunk. Although he had already reviewed my history, he wanted a few more tests done and also wanted us to return in two weeks for a final consultation.

Do any of you happen to remember that I despise the drive back and forth to MCV? The traffic around the Richmond area was horrible when I was there for my transplant in 1994, but it was much worse now and I still get car sick. Although we had to go back to Richmond a couple of times for consultations, I learned that Dr. Domson scheduled surgeries at UVA every Wednesday and I would be able to have my surgery done in Charlottesville, IF he was in agreement with Dr. Paul. Thank you, Jesus that I don't have to travel to MCV. *Philippians 4:19: "And my God will meet all your needs according to the riches of his glory in Christ Jesus."*

Dr. Domson was in total agreement with Dr. Paul, but ultimately, choosing to have the surgery would have to be my decision. You've got to be kidding…I'm not making that decision by myself. You're the professional; you're supposed to tell me what I should do.

Then, I asked Dr. Domson a loaded question: If one of your family members was in my place, what would you tell them to do? Answer: I would tell them to have the surgery. Then pretend that I am one of your family members and as Larry the Cable Guy would say -- "git r done".

Dr. Domson discussed the procedure for a hip disarticulation (an amputation through the hip joint capsule, removing the entire lower extremity) but he warned me not to be surprised if I woke up with a hemi-pelvectomy (amputation of one leg together with removal of half of the pelvis on the same side of the body). This would only be done in the event that he could not get clear margins with a disarticulation. TMI -- too much information.

A surgery date was scheduled for February 11, 2015 -- no turning back. Please understand: I have tremendous faith in God and I trust His prom-ises. He had blessed me with miracle after miracle and I knew He had a plan for my life that was far above earthly wisdom and I was not supposed to be anxious about anything, but I was terrified. In consultations with several of my doctors, I had been reminded that this surgery was going to be "huge" and it would definitely change my lifestyle forever. Please help me, Lord. *Isaiah 40:31 but those who hope in the LORD will renew their strength. They will soar on wings like eagles; they will run and not grow weary, they will walk and not be faint.*

Many of my friends were aware of my upcoming surgery and soon I received a phone call from Leecy Fink asking if she and Lesley McPhatter could arrange a prayer vigil for me. Yes, yes, yes! I couldn't have asked for more than this; to have my friends and family come together to pray. The date was set for February 10th, the night before my surgery. Leecy and Lesley had prepared a list of specific things to pray for and it would be handed out to everyone as they arrived.

When my family and I arrived at church, many of my former class-mates were already there. Some I had not seen in many years and some had even come from out of town. There were church members and my good friend, Doc Lok, and his wife, Maureen. At one point, Doc Lok pulled me aside for a little pep talk. He reminded me that God had brought me through a much bigger surgery in 1994 when I had my transplant and in his opinion, He was not through with me yet. Then we prayed together.

I will always remember that night. Everyone who was there had come with one purpose -- to pray for me. What a humbling experience! What an outpouring of love! What an answer to my prayer for help to overcome my fears! Sleep did not come easily that night.

Dr. Robert Lockridge (Doc Lok) and me

It was February 11, 2015, surgery day. The Traveling Trio was off to UVA. My surgery was scheduled for 1:00 P.M., but it was almost 4:00 before I was called. Mama and Daddy were allowed to stay with me throughout the pre-op procedures.

Soon Dr. Domson, along with his associate, Dr. Brian Werner, came into my room and said, they were ready to go. This was my first meeting with Dr. Werner, but if Dr. Domson had chosen him to assist with my surgery, I knew I was going to be in a second pair of good hands. Then, Mama asked if we could have a prayer and without hesitation, Dr. Domson and Dr. Werner joined hands with our family as we asked God's blessing for the doctors and the upcoming surgery. Then, the normal hugs and kisses and "I love you" before leaving for the O.R. Dr. Domson even rolled me to the operating room.

Around 5:00 the intercom in the waiting room announced that there was a call for Mr. or Mrs. Sirocco. Mama answered and was told my surgery had been delayed because they couldn't get an IV started and had to put a central line in my neck, but they should be getting underway soon. Wait, wait, and wait some more.

Then another phone call, this time from Dr. Domson letting my parents know that the surgery was over and I was doing fine. Praise God! Although he felt that a hemipelvectomy was needed, for various medical reasons, it could not be done, so I ended up with a hip disarticulation. Somewhere in all of that, I know this was also a "God incident".

Dr. Gregory Domson and me

Mama and Daddy were told that I would be in the recovery room for a couple of hours and they would be notified when I was taken to a room. There was also a possibility that I might spend the night in the Intensive Care Unit.

When I woke up, I realized that I was in the recovery room and overheard a conversation about moving "Sirocco" to a regular room. Good idea, guys! Soon I was on my way to a room and Mama and Daddy were there waiting for me. I was wide awake, talking, and even laughing and joking with them. Mama urged Daddy to go home to be with the boys and get a good night's rest, which he did, but she stayed.

What a night! I was in a semi-private room that was barely big enough for two beds and my roommate kept the TV blasting all night long. Mama was scrunched up in a chair right beside my bed. Needless to say, there was no sleeping, and Mama and I talked all night long.

Remember, Dr. Domson is only at UVA on Wednesdays, so Dr. Werner, his associate, came in to see me the next morning. He told me the actual surgery was picture perfect, but I had lost quite a bit of blood and would be receiving a couple of units that day. No problem.

I told Dr. Werner that I was very nauseated and didn't understand why. His reply was that it could be from the Dilaudid that was going into my IV. The what? Did you say Dilaudid? I had specifically told everyone that all opioids made me deathly sick and to please refrain from giving them to me. Tylenol would be just fine. Oh well, they thought they were doing me a favor by trying to control my pain. Once the Dilaudid was stopped, the nausea soon subsided. All's well that ends well.

It was Friday, February 13, 2015. When Dr. Werner came in that morning, I asked if I could go home. After checking my vitals and the surgery site, he said that as far as he was concerned, it would be fine, but he would have to check with Dr. Domson who would have to make the final decision.

Newsflash -- Dr. Domson discharges Sharon Sirocco from UVA. Within a forty-eight-hour time period, I had traveled to UVA, had major surgery, had a blood transfusion, been discharged, and was back home. There are no words to express how I felt to have this experience behind me and to be home once again. Thank you, Jesus. *Psalm 118:14-15 "The Lord is my strength and my defense; he has become my salvation. Shouts of joy and victory resound in the tents of the righteous: The Lord's right hand has done mighty things!"*

Dr. Brian Werner and me

CHAPTER 18

Picture Me in a Bikini

• • •

I HAVE ALWAYS BEEN TOLD: Where there's a will, there's a way and I was determined to find a way to compensate for the loss of my leg. I would just have to learn new techniques instead of doing things the usual way -- especially going to the bathroom, because now, every time I tried to sit on the commode, I would fall in. It was a comical sight and Mama and I would laugh out loud. Just think about that and the next time you sit on the commode, take a look at how your upper leg holds you up and be thankful that you have a leg.

I had only been home for two days, and there I was standing in front of the kitchen sink, on one leg, washing dishes! You would think that a new hip disartic amputee would get a little sympathy!

Three weeks later, I had a post-op appointment to have my fifty-two staples removed. Dr. Domson and Dr. Werner came in to see me. Both were well pleased with the way the incision had healed, but Dr. Domson still wanted me to have radiation therapy in the very near future. In trying to cover all the bases so I wouldn't have to make a return trip to Charlottesville, he gave me a prescription for new crutches and a new prosthesis.

Both doctors gave me a big hug and I was discharged. No return appointments would be necessary unless I encountered a problem. God truly had His healing hand upon me throughout this entire procedure. On a lighter note: I was given the name "Super Star" by Dr. Domson. I'm not 100% certain of the reason, but I'll take it.

I have always tried hard to follow my doctors' instructions, so next on my agenda would be to make an appointment with my Radiation Oncologist, Dr. Hilliard, for treatments per Dr. Domson. After my initial evaluation, she told me that working up a treatment plan was going to be a challenge since this same area had previously been radiated. It would take some time and effort. What else is new where I am concerned?

I had twenty-two treatments in the upcoming weeks at the Pearson Cancer Center, giving me an opportunity to renew friendships with some of my previous techs and to meet new ones as well.

My prescription for a new prosthesis had been tucked away in a safe place until it was needed and now it was time to pull it out. My previous prosthetists were not equipped to build a prosthesis for a hip disarticulation, so I went to Virginia Prosthetics, which was located in the same building that I had worked in previously.

I had known of Jeff Pullen for a number of years, but had never needed his professional services until now. Once again, God had led me to people who cared not only for my prosthetic needs, but who cared for me as an individual. From day one, Jeff, Eli, Sharidy, and Connie were like family. Jeff, Eli, and Sharidy were the prosthetists, and also a bunch of comedians. I don't think any one group of "professionals" had ever made me laugh so hard in all my life. Connie was the office manager and always welcomed me with a smile. I could depend on her to schedule my appointments at my convenience. She also had the task of keeping the other three in line, as if that was possible.

Can you picture me in a bikini? Didn't think so. Me neither, but I was going to get a "bikini" socket, which is the part of the prosthesis into which the stump of my hip would fit. This was a fairly new procedure and I think I might have been kind of a guinea pig for this group. Many times we laughed and laughed as they tried to turn me into a contortionist in order to make a perfect mold for my socket. Once the socket was complete, a hip, knee, ankle joint, and foot would be attached.

Soon my new leg was completely assembled and I was ready for a trial run. It took a little effort to get it on, but once I was safely buckled in (click it or ticket), I was able to take a few steps between the parallel bars. But, as the Carpenters sang...We've only just begun. Adjustments to a prosthesis are never ending, so Jeff, Eli, Sharidy, and I will be in this for the "long haul".

F.Y.I. – I was told that I needed to give my prosthesis a name, so I used the first letter of the following names: Jeff, Eli, Sharidy, Sharon -- "Jess". An appropriate name, don't you think for those who had "given birth" to her. I love you guys!

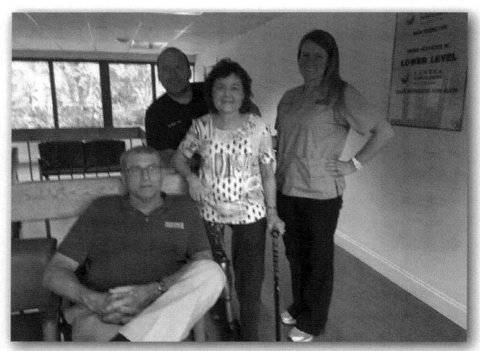

Jeff, Eli, Sharon and Sharidy

I'm here to tell you that you don't put a full prosthetic leg on and start walking immediately as I was able to do with my below the knee prosthesis. I had a new leg, but now would come the hard part -- learning how to use it properly. That's where physical therapy would come in.

As it so happened, Virginia Baptist Hospital had recently hired a new therapist who had extensive training with amputees at Duke University and she would be working with me. No coincidence – another "God incident".

We hit it off right away and although she was a slave driver, she accomplished the task of teaching me the ins and outs of how to properly use my prosthesis, such as getting up and down from a chair. Some of my attempts to follow her directions were a sight to behold and we couldn't help but laugh.

There were lots of core strengthening exercises to be learned and at the end of my session, my shirt would be soaked with sweat. The many hours we spent working together paid off and I graduated from a wheelchair, to using two crutches, then to one crutch, and finally to a cane. Thank you, my friend.

As I bring the highlights of my journey to a close, to date, I remain cancer free and with God's help, I have made tremendous strides in every aspect of my life. Although I will never be able to express the gratitude I have in my heart for each and every person mentioned in my story and many others I never met that were involved behind the scenes, let me try... thank you in Bunches and Piles and Heaps...Oh My! To God be the glory, both now and forever. *John 16:33 "I have told you these things, so that in me you may have peace. In this world you will have trouble. But take heart! I have overcome the world."*

Matthew 17:20 ...if you have faith as small as a mustard seed, you can say to this mountain, 'Move from here to there,' and it will move. Nothing will be impossible for you."

My friend,

Thank you for purchasing my book. The first and foremost reason for writing this book is to bring glory to God and secondly, to provide hope, encouragement, and an awareness of God's love, mercy, grace, healing, and miracles to you, the reader. My belief is that God has a plan and purpose for each life He has created. Most folks consider an unexplainable turn of events to be a coincidence, but I consider it to be a "God incident" -- an unexplainable event from God.

It is not a "coincidence" that you purchased this book, but a "God incident". My prayer is that His purpose will be made evident to you as you read my story. I am definitely one of His miracles and I believe that I am here today because God's purpose for my life has not been fulfilled. In other words, He ain't through with me yet!

"He performs wonders that cannot be fathomed, miracles that cannot be counted" ... Job 9:10

If you have never accepted Jesus Christ as your personal Savior, the following plan of salvation will direct you as to how you can receive forgiveness of your sins and assurance of eternal life.

1. God loves you and has a plan for you!
   The Bible says, *"God so loved the world that He gave His one and only Son, (Jesus Christ), that whoever believes in Him shall not perish, but have eternal life" (John 3:16)*. Jesus said, *"I came that they may have life and have it abundantly"* — *a complete life full of purpose (John 10:10)*.

But here's the problem:

2. Man is sinful and separated from God.
   We have all done, thought, or said bad things, which the Bible calls "sin." The Bible says, *"All have sinned and fall short of the glory of God" (Romans 3:23).*

The result of sin is death, spiritual separation from God (Romans 6:23).

The good news:

3. God sent His Son to die for your sins!
   Jesus died in our place so we could live with Him in eternity.

"God demonstrates His own love toward us, in that while we were yet sinners, Christ died for us" (Romans 5:8).

But it didn't end with His death on the cross. He rose again and still lives!

"Christ died for our sins. ... He was buried. ... He was raised on the third day, according to the Scriptures." (1 Corinthians 15:3-4).

Jesus is the only way to God. Jesus said, *"I am the way, and the truth, and the life; no one comes to the Father, but through Me" (John 14:6).*

4. Would you like to receive God's forgiveness?
   We can't earn salvation; we are saved by God's grace when we have faith in His Son, Jesus Christ. All you have to do is believe you are a sinner, that Christ died for your sins, and ask His forgiveness. Then turn from your sins -- that's called repentance. Jesus Christ knows you and loves you. What matters to Him is the attitude of your heart, your honesty. Pray a simple prayer such as the following:

"Dear Lord Jesus,

I know I am a sinner, and I ask for your forgiveness. I believe you died for my sins and rose from the dead. I trust and follow you as my Lord and Savior. Guide my life and help me to do your will. In your name, amen."

I would love for you to share with me any comments you may have about my book.

You may send them via e-mail to: BPHOM64@gmail.com

ABOUT THE AUTHOR

• • •

SHARON E. SIROCCO HAS HAD many health problems throughout her life. She was diagnosed with diabetes at a young age. She later had a kidney and pancreas transplant and went through chemotherapy, radiation therapy, and surgery to treat her cancer. She has had a hip disarticulation amputation, which is the removal of the entire leg.

Through it all, Sirocco has never lost her faith or her optimism, and she even helped to develop a spirituality health ministry with the Lynchburg Rheumatology Clinic. Despite her many health challenges, she started working at the clinic as a transcriptionist and spent twenty-five years improving her skills. She has worked as a certified coder, notary public, in-house IT expert, human-resources manager, and bookkeeper.

As a testament to her deep faith in the kindness of God, Sirocco always ends her e-mails with this simple yet profound claim: "God is good."

40558027R00064

Made in the USA
Middletown, DE
16 February 2017